Inspired

Wisdom for a Woman's Walk with Jesus

To Dianne
My dear Sunflower Sister
Love,
Barbara S. Maxwell

CLAY BRIDGES
PRESS

Barbara S Maxwell

Inspired
Wisdom for a Woman's Walk with Jesus

Jesus, this has always been your project.
You have been with me each morning, teaching me to trust you,
inspiring me to write beyond my ability.
I give this book to you!

May this book be an inspiring legacy for my daughters, Amy and Laura, for Sara,
and for my grandchildren: Collin, Logan, Emily, Lilly, Jaxon, and Mason.

Introduction

Long before I even had an idea for preparing a book of devotionals and certainly before I ever imagined this work could be published, there was simply a desire to reach out to my sister who was experiencing depression.

How could I help? Maybe just a message each morning, by text, letting her know I was thinking of her, sending my love, and asking God for a scripture to remind her that her wonderful Father in heaven cares.

I had no idea that God had more in mind for me with this small daily gesture to my sister. It started as a ministry of daily morning devotionals texted to a few women, then dozens, and now to many dozens of women. These morning thoughts even found their way passed along from friend to friend all over the country and even to other parts of the world! I am in awe at what God can do! I am astounded still at how He has helped inspire the growth of my faith through it all!

I wake up early, expectant each morning, prepare my heart, and trust that He will help me find a nugget—a scriptural message to touch the heart of even one woman that day.

I am watching with amazement what His word has done in my heart and can do in the heart of any woman who is open to receive Him. God has allowed me to be a part of this daily nourishing, and I am humbled by this each morning.

Will you carve out some time to go deeper with me? Will you trust that God is working in your life? Can you believe that He will reach in and draw out your beauty and your gifts and inspire you to grow?

Thank you for the privilege of allowing me to share with you each day.

Love in Christ,

Barbara S. Maxwell

Morning by morning he wakens me and opens my understanding to his will.
The Sovereign LORD has spoken to me, and I have listened.

—Isa. 50:4–5

Day One

The most beautiful thing we can experience is the mysterious.
It is the source of all true art and all science.

—Albert Einstein

"My thoughts are nothing like your thoughts," says the LORD.
"And my ways are far beyond anything you could imagine. For just as the
heavens are higher than the earth, so my ways are higher than your ways and
my thoughts higher than your thoughts."

—Isa. 55:8–9

I love the mysterious. I think that is why I have always found boxes so intriguing. I can imagine opening the lid and then . . . ? Not knowing what I'll find inside is what makes opening a box so exciting.

The unknowns of life can be so intriguing and often frustrating too. We try so hard to figure God out. We often try to put Him into our little boxes and close the lid and say, "I understand it all now!"

Well, just about the time we think that way, God amazes us with something so far beyond us! He is this very mysterious Creator, who both began everything and came to the earth to be our Lamb to save us from ourselves! He's the God who can heal and raise from death.

And He's the God who surprises us and delights us with the sweetest newborn baby's delicateness, the gift of intimacy with a loving spouse, and the invitation into the vast and unsearchable depths of the stars and galaxies that we gaze at in the night sky. We witness stunning sunrises and sunsets, the fireworks of a lightning storm, or the quiet of a gentle rain and marvel at the ways of this God.

Our Creator is so mysterious, so far beyond our comprehension, and yet He offers to come and dwell with us in our hearts! Christ Himself is our box opened up!

We are invited to peek inside and begin to understand the mystery of why He came. He is our path to being forgiven, He is our treasure, He is our inspiration, and He is our way to a secure future.

> *God wanted people to look for him, and perhaps in searching all around for him, they would find him. But he is not far from any of us.*
> —Acts 17:27 ERV

What is still very mysterious to you about this amazing and loving God?

Day Two

God is the friend of silence. See how nature—trees, flowers, grass—grow in silence; see the stars, the moon and the sun, how they move in silence.

—Mother Teresa

This is what the Sovereign LORD, the Holy One of Israel, says: "Only in returning to me and resting in me will you be saved. In quietness and confidence is your strength. But you would have none of it."

—Isa. 30:15

It is good to wait quietly for the LORD to save them.

—Lam. 3:26 ERV

Silence, stillness, and patience.

These are not desirable conditions for most of us. We are attracted by them but do very little to promote them. We'd like a bit of them but know that it takes time to acquire their virtues. We are just a bit too busy usually to earn them in our lives. Sometimes, I will turn off the radio in my car to find some blessed relief from the noise of talk and even music.

We have a noisy fan to sleep by, but there is such sweet silence when I finally shut it off in the morning. Even in the buzz of a gathering of friends, don't you sometimes just want to find a bit of peace?

God wants that for us too. We can't hear Him very well unless we determine to find quiet spaces in the cacophony of our days. As women, it's essential to our inner beauty to find some peace. Will we have none of it and claim busyness as our best excuse?

We can find it if we decide it's worthwhile! Whatever seems worthy to us gets our attention, doesn't it?

> *Be still, and know that I am God. I am exalted among the nations, I am exalted in the earth!*
>
> —Ps. 46:10 RSV

Will you ask God to give you a deep need for silence so you can hear Him?
Will you rearrange your schedule to find some time for silence and listening to Him?

Day Three

If there is no struggle, there is no progress.
—Frederick Douglass

Therefore if anyone is in Christ [that is, grafted in, joined to Him by faith in Him as Savior], he is a new creature [reborn and renewed by the Holy Spirit]; the old things [the previous moral and spiritual condition] have passed away. Behold, new things have come [because spiritual awakening brings a new life].
—2 Cor. 5:17 AMP

The tiny caterpillar is an amazing creature. Starting life as an egg tucked on a leaf, this little insect emerges and begins to feed on that same leaf, quickly growing and maturing. When full-grown, it begins to form the chrysalis around itself. Something miraculous is about to happen.

As this insect struggles to free itself from its cocoon, what emerges is a stunningly beautiful transformed creature completely unlike it was before. Its limbs, tissue, and organs are all changed, and what is revealed is a multicolored insect with wings, able to soar up into the sky. It can travel on a breeze discovering new vistas, no longer chained to the leaf and tree.

When we decide to put our trust in Christ, it is much like the metamorphosis of the caterpillar into a butterfly. We too make a complete transformation. We are a new creature with a new spiritual nature. Our minds are renewed, as we are indwelled by the Holy Spirit. Our life is transformed. We have power from God to soar and are able to do and be so much more than before!

We experience new vistas; we reach greater heights—places that our old selves could never even imagine. God can transform anyone this way. It's an exciting process to move from having confidence in ourselves to trusting in the transforming life of Jesus our Savior. And like the butterfly, it is an amazing metamorphosis!

> *So all of us who have had that veil removed can see and reflect the glory of the Lord. And the Lord—who is the Spirit—makes us more and more like him as we are changed into his glorious image.*
>
> —2 Cor. 3:18

Have you experienced this glorious transformation in your life?

Day Four

*Love takes off masks that we fear we cannot live without
and know we cannot live within.*

—James Baldwin

*Love from the center of who you are; don't fake it.
Run for dear life from evil; hold on for dear life to good.*

—Rom. 12:9–10 MSG

Authenticity is a challenge in a world where perfection, beauty, fame, and popularity are worshipped so much!

I try to be genuine, but I have had enough of a struggle with self-consciousness to understand the difficult path we walk as women. Today, may I ask: Do you still wear a mask? Are you able to be authentic and relaxed and yourself in anyone's company?

The path I took to remove my mask began with the profound realization that I was of value to my God. Before that, my first thoughts were of my value in the eyes of others. And I always fell short in looks, in talent, and in accomplishment.

But when it finally sank in that God really loves me and sees me in Christ as being perfect and important and very special, then what others thought became much less powerful to me. I could begin to relax, to live fully, and to be myself—foibles and all.

> *Oh yes, you shaped me first inside, then out; you formed me in my mother's womb. I thank you, High God—you're breathtaking! Body and soul, I am marvelously made! I worship in adoration—what a creation! You know me inside and out, you know every bone in my body; you know exactly how I was made, bit by bit, how I was sculpted from nothing into something. Like an open book, you watched me grow from conception to birth; all the stages of my life were spread out before you, the days of my life all prepared before I'd even lived one day.*
> —Ps.139:13–16 MSG

> *"You didn't choose me, remember; I chose you, and put you in the world to bear fruit, fruit that won't spoil. As fruit bearers, whatever you ask the Father in relation to me, he gives you."*
> —John 15:16 MSG

He chose you! He chose me! No need for masks today!
Is it difficult for you to live without a mask?

Day Five

You usually have to wait for that which is worth waiting for.
—Craig Bruce

We wait!
We wait for results.
We wait for things to happen.
We wait for it to be over.
We wait for it to start.
We wait for morning.
We wait for sleep to come.

We wait for a child.
We wait for a child to learn.
We wait for growth.
We wait in lines.
We wait for appointments.
We wait in prayer for God to act!

That is why I wait expectantly, trusting God to help, for he has promised. I long for him more than sentinels long for the dawn. O Israel, hope in the Lord; for he is loving and kind and comes to us with armloads of salvation.

—Ps. 130:5–7 TLB

But, do we ever think that God waits for us?

God waits for us to take a step.

God waits for us to learn.

He waits for us to be ready for something good.

He waits for us to mature.

He waits for us to pray for others.

He waits for us to cry out to Him for help!

So the Lord must wait for you to come to him so he can show you his love and compassion. For the Lord is a faithful God. Blessed are those who wait for his help.

—Isa. 30:18

Yet I am confident I will see the Lord's goodness while I am here in the land of the living. Wait patiently for the Lord. Be brave and courageous. Yes, wait patiently for the Lord.

—Ps. 27:13–14

What are you waiting prayerfully for right now?

Day Six

The house does not rest upon the ground, but upon a woman.
—Mexican Proverb

A wise woman builds her home, but a foolish woman tears
it down with her own hands.
—Prov. 14:1

Do you stop to give credit to the tremendous power and control that you as a woman have over your home, your relationships, and your world?

Whether you are on your own, have a husband, raise children, have a career, volunteer, or all of the above as many women do, your words and actions can create a haven of peace, or they can bring disorder to a space by the way you handle things!

As women, we have great influence, creative power, and loving arms that can make it all better. With our eye for color and detail and our knack for lovely creativity, we bring softness to our hearths, others' hearts, and our worlds.

We may teach, earn an income, cook, clean, nurse, love, comfort and counsel, and even nurture life throughout our days. The list goes on, and our roles never really end, do they?

Even when we are older, we are a friend, an encourager, a helpmate, grandmother, aunt, caretaker, and often a safe place to land in times of woe! I pray for each of you, and for myself, to never give up asking God to help us be the very best as women!

> *Who can find a virtuous and capable wife? She is more precious than rubies. . . . Charm is deceptive, and beauty does not last; but a woman who fears the* Lord *will be greatly praised. Reward her for all she has done. Let her deeds publicly declare her praise.*
>
> —Prov. 31:10, 30–31

How can you increase your awareness and effectiveness as a woman in your world?

Day Seven

Happiness is not a matter of events, it depends upon the tides of the mind.
—Alice Meynell

Those who listen to instruction will prosper;
those who trust the LORD will be joyful.
—Prov. 16:20

Do you find yourself dwelling on your feelings as you start your day? If you are prone to that, do you find that your feelings dictate how your day goes? This tendency will keep our emotions as capricious as the changing tides in the ocean.

Do you allow the weather to control how you feel on any given day? Do you let other people's whims determine whether you are able to be at peace? Many people do so without thinking.

The mind and our thoughts are the entry point to true joy and peace. Our peace and joy come from how we manage the first thoughts that enter our minds in the morning! If you want to be a peace-filled person, getting hold of your first thoughts will be the key to making that happen.

Watch out for the negative thought, the lie, the worry, the fearful thought, or doubts. We stop them in their tracks at the door of our mind! We do not let them enter. We don't invite them in to stay. We don't entertain them like a guest, as though invited! We see them for what they are: enemies of our peace!

We run to the Counselor of our thoughts, the Holy Spirit, for the truth! We ask for strength to keep the door firmly closed to invader thoughts, such as worry and fear, that come to rob us of much-needed peace and joy! We seek the truth from our God and His Word!

> *You will keep in perfect peace all who trust in you, all whose thoughts are fixed on you! Trust in the LORD always, for the LORD GOD is the eternal Rock.*
> —Isa. 26:3–4

Can you examine your guest list and see who you are inviting into your mind to stay?

Day Eight

Everything passes, everything breaks, everything wearies.
—French Proverb

I have told you all this so that you may have peace in me.
Here on earth you will have many trials and sorrows. But take heart,
because I have overcome the world.

—John 16:33

Life can be challenging, and we all have been forewarned that in life we'll have some tough times! Is it hard for us to accept that troubles can happen to everyone? Is it hard to have faith when things go wrong with our well-laid-out plans?

If we can just hold on! If we could only trust! If we could know that God is there for us and with us in each trial, then maybe, just maybe, we could hold on a little longer and not give up!

Any one of us could preach a sermon on these subjects—trouble, heartache, and the silence of waiting—couldn't we? Do we remember how we got through trouble the last time?

Could it have been better handled if we had known then what we know now—that things finally do calm down, that we do recover from the worst of it all, and that we can learn to adjust to loss, somewhat? We can even go on and live fully again after a while.

Can we allow God to hold us up, carry us through, and even rise above our circumstances the next time?

> *And, after you have suffered for a little while, the God of all grace who called you to his eternal glory in Christ will himself restore, confirm, strengthen, and establish you. To him belongs the power forever. Amen.*
>
> —1 Pet. 5:10–11 (NET)

Will you hold on in trust just a bit longer?
Can you hold tight to God's hand to pull you through?

Day Nine

Worry never robs tomorrow of its sorrow, it only saps today of its joy.
—Leo Buscaglia

*"So don't be anxious about tomorrow. God will take care of your tomorrow too.
Live one day at a time."*
—Matt. 6:34 TLB

I was a tomboy growing up in a time when cowboy movies were really popular. I remember seeing the long, dusty cattle drives. Moving those steers to market was a very big deal!

Those seasoned cowboys would all mount up and ride alongside the herd keeping watch over all the animals to make sure they didn't lose a single one. Each steer was very important to them—each one costly. One stray animal could slow them

down and cause delay, hampering their progress and possibly leading the whole herd into trouble.

Our thought life is a lot like that: Whenever one of our thoughts goes astray, we should lasso it and "steer" it back into submission. Our thoughts are important and costly; they govern our choices and actions. If we don't want our thoughts to distract us and hamper our progress, we must care about how we think.

> *Temptation is the pull of man's own evil thoughts and wishes. These evil thoughts lead to evil actions and afterwards to the death penalty from God. So don't be misled, dear brothers. But whatever is good and perfect comes to us from God, the Creator of all light, and he shines forever without change or shadow.*
>
> —James 1:14–17 TLB

So today, let's steer our thoughts away from the temptation to worry. Let's, instead, "corral" our worries over to God, "herding" them all safely into our prayer life.

With our minds focused on thankfulness, we can "gallop" through our day with joy!

"Head 'em up, move 'em out!"

What causes you to go astray in your thought life?

Day Ten

Fear can keep us up all night long, but faith makes one fine pillow.
—Philip Gulley

Clothed in strength and dignity, with nothing to fear,
she smiles when she thinks about the future.
—Prov. 31:25 VOICE

If we are going to be successful living by faith, we must face our fears!
    If it's people we fear, is it their approval we crave?
    If it's authority we fear, is it failure in their eyes that paralyzes us?
    Is it circumstances we fear because we can't surmount them?
    Is it our own health that frightens us because we are out of control?

If you fear other people, you are walking into a dangerous trap; but if you
trust in the Eternal, you will be safe.
—Prov. 29:25 VOICE

Yes, believe me, I know there are a great many things that can cause us to fear. Certainly, we have a right to our feelings about the real problems and crises looming over our heads. Even then, God tells us not to fear and not to worry!

Maybe, just maybe, if we change what we are focusing on, then we might just get a handle on this fear! If we could begin to rely on Him, what a difference that could make. Each time we allow fear to overwhelm our hearts, we are making a choice!

Next time, can we try to make a new choice? Let's grab on to God's hand at each turn of our emotions.

Faith needs practice.

Fear puts focus on our problem.

Faith is the practice of putting our focus on our God, the problem-solver!

> *God is our shelter and our strength. When troubles seem near, God is nearer, and He's ready to help. So why run and hide? No fear, no pacing, no biting fingernails. When the earth spins out of control, we are sure and fearless. When mountains crumble and the waters run wild, we are sure and fearless. Even in heavy winds and huge waves, or as mountains shake, we are sure and fearless. . . . "Be still, be calm, see, and understand I am the True God. I am honored among all the nations. I am honored over all the earth."*
> —Ps. 46:1–3,10 VOICE

Which will you choose to focus on: Fear or faith in your sheltering God?

Day Eleven

A fool and his money are soon parted.
—English Proverb

Then he said, "Beware! Guard against every kind of greed.
Life is not measured by how much you own."
—Luke 12:15

God blesses each of us with unique qualities and gifts that He wants us to use for His glory reflected in our lives!

Wealth is a gift. But, in the wrong hands it can be a real temptation to squander it. It's all in how we see our abundance.

Sadly, when money suddenly lands in their laps, most lottery winners do not know what to do with it, and within a few years, almost all of them have let it slip through their fingers.

> *For the love of money is the root of all kinds of evil. And some people, craving money, have wandered from the true faith and pierced themselves with many sorrows.*
>
> —1 Tim. 6:10

This truth isn't just about money, is it? It applies to any gift, bounty, blessing, or talent that we misuse or fail to develop or squander or bury instead of developing the potential. As we examine ourselves this day, may we validate the gifts and blessings we have been given. Thank God for them and develop them for His glory.

It's a good reminder to ask God to help us get back into the proper attitude and appreciate the blessings we've been given.

> *The LORD is my chosen portion and my cup; you hold my lot. The lines have fallen for me in pleasant places; indeed, I have a beautiful inheritance.*
>
> —Ps. 16:5–6 ESV

Are you content? Have any of your blessings become a distraction to you?

Day Twelve

Let your mind be like a tightly woven net to catch emotions and feelings that come, and investigate them before you react.

—Ajahn Chah

Understand this, my dear brothers and sisters: You must all be quick to listen, slow to speak, and slow to get angry. Human anger does not produce the righteousness God desires.

—James 1:19–20

We often hear wrongly, react too quickly, sin too readily with our misunderstandings, impatience, and lack of love toward those around us. We even use this as justification to make selfish choices. We hurt others, and we regret so much!

Today, can we make a fresh start? Can we resolve to take responsibility for our thoughts and actions? We do have self-control because God can give it to us.

We can hold back our snap reactions because God can equip us with patience. We can give grace because God can remind us of the truth about ourselves. He can give us the wisdom to take what we hear with grace and believe the best about people.

If we can change the way we think, it will certainly lead to a change in our behavior.

> *Don't copy the behavior and customs of this world, but let God transform you into a new person by changing the way you think. Then you will learn to know God's will for you, which is good and pleasing and perfect.*
> —Rom. 12:2

> *And now, dear brothers and sisters, one final thing. Fix your thoughts on what is true, and honorable, and right, and pure, and lovely, and admirable. Think about things that are excellent and worthy of praise.*
> —Phil. 4:8

How can you be more positive and generous in your thought life toward other people?

Day Thirteen

A man who finds no satisfaction in himself will seek for it in vain elsewhere.
—La Rochefoucauld

The LORD is my shepherd; I have all that I need. He lets me rest in green meadows; he leads me beside peaceful streams. He renews my strength. He guides me along right paths, bringing honor to his name. Even when I walk through the darkest valley, I will not be afraid, for you are close beside me. Your rod and your staff protect and comfort me.

—Ps. 23:1–4

We can search the world over, shop for days and days, spin our wheels in endless activity, strive and strive with very little result, or wander through our days ticking off lists. But, without a true meaning and purpose that God has designed for

us, we can look in the mirror and realize we have no real peace in our hearts or rest for our souls.

What if we, as women, allow God to guide our mornings, watch over our nights, and arm our days with purpose for Him?

What if we value what He values, slow down a bit, and think a bit more about what God wants? Then, I believe we will have peace.

We can set our sights on what God sets before us: this wonderful life lived one day at a time with Him, followed by our true reward in the future. This perspective will keep us from senseless striving and purposeless activity.

> *Better is the sight of the eyes than the wandering of the appetite: this also is vanity and a striving after wind.*
>
> —Eccles. 6:9 ESV

> *Finally, believers, rejoice! Be made complete [be what you should be], be comforted, be like-minded, live in peace [enjoy the spiritual well-being experienced by believers who walk closely with God]; and the God of love and peace [the source of lovingkindness] will be with you.*
>
> —2 Cor. 13:11 AMP

Is there striving and emptiness in any of your goals or activities that may need a fresh look?

Day Fourteen

He who divides and shares is left with the best share.
—Mexican Proverb

Give, and you will receive. Your gift will return to you in full—pressed down, shaken together to make room for more, running over, and poured into your lap. The amount you give will determine the amount you get back.

—Luke 6:38

We instinctively test our children when they are young to see where their hearts are when it comes to sharing. We ask them, "May I have a berry, or a french fry, or a bite?"

We want our children to learn the joy and reward of sharing, don't we? It upsets us if they are possessive because we see that they don't understand that we bought

the things they have for them or gave them what they are enjoying. They may not have the incentive to share with the giver. We continue to test them and give them another chance to see how good it feels to share—how much joy it brings us when they finally share on their own!

Today, may we examine ourselves and test our giving natures. Do we understand that our possessions have all been given to us and that God wants us to overflow with generosity back to Him by sharing with others? Our Parent want us to know the joy and the discipline of releasing a "french fry" back into His hand!

> *Honor the L*ORD *with your wealth and with the best part of everything you produce. Then he will fill your barns with grain, and your vats will overflow with good wine.*
>
> —Prov. 3:9–10

> *And this same God who takes care of me will supply all your needs from his glorious riches, which have been given to us in Christ Jesus. Now all glory to God our Father forever and ever! Amen.*
>
> —Phil. 4:19–20

How generous are you with the blessings that God has given you?

Day Fifteen

When you change the way you look at things,
the things you look at change.

—Albert Einstein

Do not be conformed to this world, but be transformed by the renewal
of your mind, that by testing you may discern what is the will of God,
what is good and acceptable and perfect.

—Rom. 12:2 ESV

Every day, we have many ups and downs, little tensions, and circumstances that are uniquely ours. They sometimes overwhelm us in the moment with fear or paralysis.

I wonder, do we always pray to be delivered out of our troubles? What if instead of making a desperate cry, we pray to find the strength to stand up in our troubles and learn from our trial and be better at the end of it? Then, would we grow up a bit more in our faith and be more trusting of God after it all was done? Could we even find ourselves rejoicing when we look back at the struggle? Wouldn't it be wonderful if we grew through each of life's hurdles?

We might even be an inspiration to someone else watching how we handle those tough moments that we find ourselves going through.

God can open up the way, be our strength, and build our faith when we recognize the potential in the difficulties of our life!

> *And we all, with unveiled face, beholding the glory of the Lord, are being transformed into the same image from one degree of glory to another. For this comes from the Lord who is the Spirit.*
>
> —2 Cor. 3:18 ESV

How can you begin to see your circumstances as opportunities for faith-building and transformation?

Day Sixteen

Failure is not falling down but refusing to get up.
—Robert Schuller

When little children fall, they usually cry out and reach up for a hand, a comforting pat, or a healing kiss from their parent to make it all better, to rescue them, and to help them. What happens to change all that for us as adult women?

When we fall down, we struggle alone to get up; our pride kicks in, and embarrassment takes over. Often, if a fall is from despair or loss, we may just lie in our beds not wanting to face the day or go on in our lives. If it's temptation, we struggle alone and often give in!

Unless we are seriously injured, we are mortified at a trip or fall. We don't see it as just part of life's challenges, and we certainly don't want the toughening experience that it should bring!

A small child is not aware, but her parents are very aware that falling and getting up is part of the "exercise" that makes a child both physically and emotionally stronger, more resilient, and more careful in the future. A child seems to sense and be assured that their parent is near so that she cries out for help at every turn.

What do we do when falls, temptation, struggles, and surprises come? Do we cry out to our Parent to rescue us and help us up? Do we feel God's loving presence near us, ready to put out a hand to lift us off the floor or out of the pit? He can even help us clean up our messes, and He also offers a protective push to save us from life's temptations.

The LORD helps the fallen and lifts those bent beneath their loads.
—Ps. 145:14

As for me, I look to the LORD for help. I wait confidently for God to save me, and my God will certainly hear me. Do not gloat over me, my enemies! For though I fall, I will rise again. Though I sit in darkness, the LORD will be my light.
—Mic. 7:7–8

Are you more inclined to endure it alone, or do you ask God for His help when you fall?

Day Seventeen

Faith is taking the first step even when you don't see the whole staircase.
—Martin Luther King Jr.

He told them another parable: "The kingdom of heaven is like a
mustard seed, which a man took and planted in his field.
Though it is the smallest of all seeds, yet when it grows,
it is the largest of garden plants and becomes a tree,
so that the birds come and perch in its branches."
—Matt. 13:31–32 NIV

It started with a tiny mustard seed, common and small. When that seed was planted in the ground, it grew into a very sturdy treelike plant.

Have you ever thought about how little faith it really takes to begin something? Is there just a bit of faith, not in yourself, but faith to believe God is there in a new undertaking? Can you believe that God is actively involved with you, and that He is just waiting to see that seed of faith in your heart?

Is it impossible for you to believe that the impossible can happen—that people might change a bit for the better; that I can change; that the miraculous can occur; that my life can get better; or that I can even grow in confidence and strength?

Can we revisit faith today? Lord, test us! Is our faith strong or weak? Remember, just a little seed of faith in God can make all the difference!

> *The fundamental fact of existence is that this trust in God, this faith, is the firm foundation under everything that makes life worth living. It's our handle on what we can't see. The act of faith is what distinguished our ancestors, set them above the crowd.*
>
> —Heb. 11:1–2 MSG

Is there a struggle in your day for which just a seed of faith in God's power might make all the difference?

Day Eighteen

*When one door of happiness closes, another opens; but often we look so long at
the closed door that we do not see the one which has opened for us.*

—Helen Keller

Have you had the door shut in your face—the door of happiness?
You're going through a tough time. Maybe someone has disappointed you,
you've lost someone close to you, an opportunity was taken away, or you've felt
rejection from a close friend? What then?

I believe that each day will be much better when we accept that people are fragile
and that they will fail us at some point. Even those closest to us are not perfect, and
we ourselves are going to fail others!

Sometimes, we expect too much, or we don't deal well with losses or conflict.
Things often just build up to a crisis, and then the fallout happens! We disappoint
each other!

For I know the plans I have for you, says the LORD, plans for welfare and not for evil, to give you a future and a hope.

—Jer. 29:11 (RSV)

The one whom we can always depend on is our God! He is forever there, without fail, your constant companion, if you let Him be.

He is stronger than your problems and able to lift you out of your mess. Be confident. Believe. Cry out to Him. He is faithful and will deliver you!

Have you never heard? Have you never understood? The LORD is the everlasting God, the Creator of all the earth. He never grows weak or weary. No one can measure the depths of his understanding. He gives power to the weak and strength to the powerless. Even youths will become weak and tired, and young men will fall in exhaustion. But those who trust in the LORD will find new strength. They will soar high on wings like eagles. They will run and not grow weary. They will walk and not faint.

—Isa. 40:28–31

Is there a circumstance in your life today for which trusting more in God and less in fragile people would help?

Day Nineteen

*One of the effects of fear is to disturb the senses and cause things
to appear other than what they are.*

—Miguel de Cervantes

*Even when I walk through the darkest valley, I will not be afraid, for you are
close beside me. Your rod and your staff protect and comfort me.*

—Ps. 23:4

Fear can be very debilitating!

It starts in early childhood, especially in the dark. In the night, our minds create monsters out of shadows. As I grew up watching television, my nightmares centered around alligators and quicksand! I couldn't allow my foot to hang over the edge of my bed for fear of those reptiles!

It all seems rather silly to me now—that I was ever afraid of those things. But, at the time, my fears kept me from much-needed rest! Do your fears keep you from restorative sleep?

Both real and imagined scenarios can frighten us and cause us to tremble and lose our faith in those moments. How can we live victoriously with all those fears bombarding us?

Fighting the fear-fight with the right weapons is paramount. If we understand the spiritual battle going on in the unseen world, then prayer becomes more important to us. When fear approaches our door, knock on God's door! Pray fervently to Him. Tell our Father all about it. He'll open the door and unleash His mighty warriors to battle fear and the darkness; He will keep us firmly in His arms held above the fray!

> *I prayed to the LORD, and he answered me. He freed me from all my fears.*
> *Those who look to him for help will be radiant with joy; no shadow of shame*
> *will darken their faces. In my desperation I prayed, and the LORD listened;*
> *he saved me from all my troubles. For the angel of the LORD is a guard; he*
> *surrounds and defends all who fear him.*
>
> Ps. 34:4–7

What can you bring to God that has you in its grip of fear right now?

Day Twenty

A person starts to live when he can live outside himself.
—Albert Einstein

I remember the frustration early in my adulthood of wanting to be a kind and loving person as I knew I was supposed to be.

I would envy the seemingly natural response I noticed in others when it came to their hurting friends—the effective way they responded during the sickness or tragedy around them.

I wondered why that impulse didn't come from inside my heart. Oh yes, I could try, and I did try to model after them.

I could copy the behavior, but I knew down deep something was amiss, something wasn't there, that I wanted to be there, in me!

Dear friends, let us love one another, for love comes from God. Everyone who loves has been born of God and knows God. Whoever does not love does not know God, because God is love. This is how God showed his love among us: He sent his one and only Son into the world that we might live through him. This is love: not that we loved God, but that he loved us and sent his Son as an atoning sacrifice for our sins. Dear friends, since God so loved us, we also ought to love one another. No one has ever seen God; but if we love one another, God lives in us and his love is made complete in us.

—1 John 4:7–12 NIV

Well, now I understand that the success of love is the journey to know God. I had it all backward and sideways. First choose to seek God, recognizing that without Christ, it is impossible to love from the inside out.

With Christ as my Savior, I am equipped to bear the fruit of the Holy Spirit: love, joy, peace, patience, kindness, gentleness . . . these will overflow from within.

What a transformation it can make in our lives when we let go and be led by Christ! Jesus showed us what real love was when He laid down His life for us. He asks in return, not that we give up our lives, although many have, but that we live a life of love and follow His lead.

Are you beginning to get it? Are you starting to understand what love really is?

Day Twenty-One

And in the end, it's not the years in your life that count.
It's the life in your years.
—Abraham Lincoln

For I am convinced that nothing can ever separate us from his love.
Death can't, and life can't. The angels won't, and all the powers of
hell itself cannot keep God's love away. Our fears for today,
our worries about tomorrow, or where we are—high above the sky,
or in the deepest ocean—nothing will ever be able to separate us
from the love of God demonstrated by our LORD Jesus Christ
when he died for us.
—Romans 8:38–39 TLB

How can I fail to live with excitement, with purpose, with joy, with song, with hope, and with determination in response to the knowledge that nothing can ever separate me from my God?

Oh yes, I do know why I fail sometimes. I forget. We forget, don't we, to realize that He is there with us?

Maybe we forget because we are having a tough time accepting and dealing with those difficult, often disappointing, parts of God's will for our paths.

Life can do that to us—cause us to forget all the great and wonderful things about belonging to Christ: life, hope, joy, peace, companionship, and help in times of trouble, to name just a few.

Sometimes, my memory fails me in this way. I become shortsighted to the blessings He gives that are mine. I'm praying that I remember, so my life can be full.

> *You lead me in the path of life; I experience absolute joy in your presence; you always give me sheer delight.*
>
> —Ps. 16:11 NET

What is getting in the way of having joy and delight in your day today?

Day Twenty-Two

Do I prefer to grow up and relate to life directly,
or do I choose to live and die in fear?

—Pema Chödrön

For I, the LORD *your God,*
hold your right hand; it is I who say to you,
"Fear not, I will help you."

—Isa. 41:13 RSV

I am not unsympathetic to the fears that others share with me. Oh, no, I've been there, in that grip, more times than I want to remember. One very palpable time of fear I experienced was scuba diving a shipwreck, down at 100 feet. The depth alone was dramatic. The feel of the whirling current whipping around

the outer edges of the wreck and the rhythmic, haunting sound of my own breathing were my only companions.

In those moments, I felt completely isolated and alone! Fear and the beginnings of panic crept in. I began to list all the dire possibilities of my circumstances. I knew I could not quickly surface without injuring my lungs. I might hyperventilate and pass out, or I could drift away from the group.

All these thoughts began to overtake any common sense. I have never felt so helpless and so frightened as I did in those moments. It took everything in me to begin to talk myself off the ledge of panic.

I prayed and asked God for strength not to lose it. I tried to think out what was true and what wasn't. Was not my God with me here as much as on dry land?

My breathing began to slow, and the moments of fear and panic passed as I realized that this was such a beautiful and expensive chance to be there on this adventure.

I'm so glad I didn't abort that dive.

> *It is the* Lord *who goes before you; he will be with you, he will not fail you or forsake you; do not fear or be dismayed.*
>
> —Deut. 31:8 RSV

Is there some fear that has you in its grip right now? Can you call on the Lord and accept His comforting help?

Day Twenty-Three

Wherever we look upon this earth, the opportunities take shape within the problems.

—Nelson A. Rockefeller

Ask, and it will be given you; seek, and you will find; knock, and it will be opened to you.

—Matt. 7:7 RSV

When times are smooth and tranquil, our tendency is not to rock the boat. When times bring hurdles and problems, then we see the need to fix and make some changes. If everything seems fine, then we are fine. But what may be a problem is the very fact that we are more unobservant, failing to notice things right in front of our noses. Why mess with a pretty good thing?

Our children may be quietly in bad patterns. But, until the school calls or we find them searching the dark web or getting into trouble with friends, we imagine all is well.

Marriages have broken up and spouses are shocked to realize that serious issues had never been voiced.

We sail along with poor health habits, imagining we can get away with them, that is, until our test results come back.

In the end, we can actually thank God for our struggles. Problems wake us up, bring us to our knees in prayer and help us see the need to ask for help to find solutions. We also become aware, once again, of our deep dependence on our God.

We can rejoice in the middle of a disaster because God is so alive in our hearts; his rock-solid presence is once again our hope, and His provision is once again the most important thing to us!

> *Trust in the LORD with all your heart, and do not rely on your own insight.*
> *In all your ways acknowledge him and he will make straight your paths.*
> —Prov. 3:5–6 RSV

What problem do you need to ask God for His miraculous intervention?

Day Twenty-Four

Beware the barrenness of a busy life.
—Socrates

Come to me, all who labor and are heavy laden, and I will give you rest.
Take my yoke upon you, and learn from me; for I am gentle and
lowly in heart, and you will find rest for your souls.
For my yoke is easy, and my burden is light.
—Matt. 11:28–30 RSV

So many of us measure our worth by how busy we are each day. A long list of to-dos must make us feel valuable and validated. If our calendars are filled with activities, we are happy and excited about life.

What happens when our days are not full of activity? Do we feel any less valuable? Can we not see the purpose of rest, the need for prayer time, the value of contemplation, and the skill that waiting time gives?

God's still, quiet voice can be heard only when we slow down and listen! The beach at sunset can sure stop us in our tracks. Those moments tell us how important contemplation can be.

The antics of a small child will keep our attention for hours, won't they? We feel calmed and joyful as we pause to watch.

Why not intentionally pull over, carve out some downtime of contemplation, prayer, and scripture reading to calm our spirits, maybe even daily.

Our lives will be better for it! We will be healthier for it! God will be glorified through it!

> *But seek first the kingdom of God and his righteousness, and all these things will be added to you.*
>
> —Matt. 6:33 ESV

Can you take a fresh look at how you are measuring your day?

Day Twenty-Five

You can't help getting older, but you don't have to get old.
—George Burns

Gray hair is a crown of glory; it is gained by living a godly life.
—Prov. 16:31

People talk about the Golden Years, the years when we get older and, for most, set aside the careers and vocations we have spent our lives doing.

I look around at women who are retired and aging, and I say that although we age, many do not get better with time.

There are those who play all the time and seem to be about little else other than pleasure. Others seem to have only bitter complaints, and there are those who are thoughtful and industrious and useful in their aging years.

Our attitudes about growing older and our motivation to be a useful part of our families, our communities, and our churches will make all the difference in how we handle the inevitable march of time that affects us all.

In fact, God promises us a good life if we stay close to Him and useful in His hands throughout our lives:

> *But the godly will flourish like palm trees and grow strong like the cedars of Lebanon. For they are transplanted to the LORD's own house. They flourish in the courts of our God. Even in old age they will still produce fruit; they will remain vital and green. They will declare, "The LORD is just! He is my rock! There is no evil in him!"*
>
> —Ps. 92:12–15

> *I will be your God throughout your lifetime—until your hair is white with age. I made you, and I will care for you. I will carry you along and save you.*
>
> —Isa. 46:4

Let's look at aging as a gift given to us!

Today, can you pray to stay useful to God and others as you age, trusting in Him throughout your life?

Day Twenty-Six

Love unlocks doors and opens windows that weren't even there before.
—Mignon McLaughlin

It's so easy to love, isn't it?

Well, I love my husband, but am I patient with him? I love my neighbor, but do I show kindness when things heat up at a board meeting? I love my friends, but am I envious of their stuff or their abilities that I lack?

Do I really love by listening to others, or rather, do I rudely interrupt to add what I think? Love is much more complex than assigning warm feelings. Love is not really love if we fail to follow through on the actions of love.

Love endures with patience and serenity, love is kind and thoughtful, and is not jealous or envious; love does not brag and is not proud or arrogant. It is not rude; it is not self-seeking, it is not provoked [nor overly sensitive and easily angered]; it does not take into account a wrong endured. It does not rejoice at injustice, but rejoices with the truth [when right and truth prevail]. Love bears all things [regardless of what comes], believes all things [looking for the best in each one], hopes all things [remaining steadfast during difficult times], endures all things [without weakening]. Love never fails [it never fades nor ends].

—1 Cor. 13:4–8 AMP

Often, we use other people as our standard of love. We say we are far more kind than that person. We do more good works than they do. Why not use the highest standard of love, Jesus?

He showed us what love really is when He laid His life down for us even though we did not deserve such love. Now, how loving am I by that test of love? That kind of love bridges divides of hate and heals wounds of hurt and invites people into relationships.

How can you have the kind of love that Jesus showed us, that can unlock doors and open windows that were not even there before?

Day Twenty-Seven

A smiling face is half the meal.
—Latvian Proverb

A glad heart makes a happy face; a broken heart crushes the spirit. . . .
For the despondent, every day brings trouble; for the happy heart,
life is a continual feast.

—Prov. 15:13, 15

There was a time when my smile hid pain and insecurity. It was an effective mask to keep people from knowing the real me. It was the trained response I would don in every situation.

Underneath, I was not whole! I knew it, and God knew it, but it was a pretty good filter so that no one else could peek into the real me.

As a face is reflected in water, so the heart reflects the real person.

—Prov. 27:19

How's your smile? Thankfully, mine is a more genuine reflection of the inner peace I feel now. I'm so grateful that God has healed me and helped me find joy in even the smallest details of life.

Who couldn't smile genuinely at their grandchild or at the happiness of their daughters' marriages or their successes in life? Who isn't joyful at the love of their spouse or the deep friendships they share? Who couldn't smile at just about everyone, hoping to encourage their frown to turn upside down?

There are a lot of hurting people who need us—not to give them what they deserve—but to return their expressions with a big smile that just might change their day! Try a smile on for your spouse, your neighbors, your friends, or a stranger!

Let's not be sparing with this gift. It's so easy to share! Let it come from the joy deep in our hearts! God is smiling down on His children. We can reflect Him, and our hearts will overflow with a happy smile!

> *Always be full of joy in the Lord; I say it again, rejoice! Let everyone see that you are unselfish and considerate in all you do. Remember that the Lord is coming soon.*
>
> —Phil. 4:4–5 TLB

Is your smile genuine?

Day Twenty-Eight

Beauty without grace is the hook without the bait.
—Ralph Waldo Emerson

Charm can be deceptive and beauty doesn't last, but a woman who fears and reverences God shall be greatly praised.
—Prov. 31:30 TLB

We strive all our lives to measure up to those standards that our world has about beauty. No matter what we have done to promote or improve or alter or change or fix our appearance, aging occurs. If we have depended too much on our value and essence coming from our outer beauty, then we will certainly become insecure as we age.

God is lovingly teaching us, the women He so perfectly fashioned as He wanted us to be, to focus instead on changing and improving our inner beauty. This will not fade. In fact, your beauty will glow outward from within at every age if you concentrate more on building your intimate life with Him.

His joy and His closeness will cause you to be radiant, to glow, to smile joyfully—to appear as He designed you to be—perfect for Him!

> *It is not fancy hair, gold jewelry, or fine clothes that should make you beautiful. No, your beauty should come from inside you—the beauty of a gentle and quiet spirit. That beauty will never disappear. It is worth very much to God.*
> —1 Pet. 3:3–4 ERV

> *How beautiful you are, my love, how beautiful! . . . You are so beautiful, my love, in every part of you.*
> —Song of Sol. 4:1, 7 TLB

May we seek God's presence, His acceptance, and His love as we strive for the inner beauty.

In what ways has the world's view of beauty affected you?

Day Twenty-Nine

*Our belief at the beginning of a doubtful undertaking is the one thing that
ensures the successful outcome of our venture.*
—William James

For nothing will be impossible with God.
—Luke 1:37 ESV

I have to admit to doubting that some people will ever want to change for the better. I have often looked with my own eyes and concluded that they are beyond hope! I have assumed that these difficult people are a lost cause when it comes to growing less prideful, becoming humble, listening and learning, taking direction, or being more agreeable.

I've written them off with my limited view of things. I've considered them beyond prayer and beyond even changes God could make! Have you ever felt that way about anyone?

I'm beginning to learn though that my view is very narrow and cloudy and unaware of God's will and plan. For me to write someone off is just as prideful and stubborn and misguided as my estimation of them!

> *Trust in the LORD with all your heart, and do not rely on your own insight.*
> *In all your ways acknowledge him, and he will make straight your paths.*
> —Prov. 3:5–6 RSV

God has been opening my eyes lately to see things more clearly: "Is anything too hard for the LORD" (Genesis 18:14 ESV)?

Now, I can believe in what before seemed impossible. After all, I know I have been transformed in ways that someone in my past might have thought would never happen! And I have witnessed seemingly impossible transformations in others as well.

So, I am beginning to understand why God asks us to love, forgive, and keep loving and forgiving. Because there is always hope! There is always that spark of the miraculous right around the dark corner if we are willing to keep hoping and praying fervently for each one on our lists.

Is there anyone that you have struggled to believe could change—someone for whom you have carried a burden of prayer? Do you believe that, even in that situation, nothing is impossible with God?

Day Thirty

A gem is not perfected without friction, nor a man perfected without trials.
—Lucius Annaeus Seneca

*Do not be conformed to this world but be transformed by the
renewal of your mind, that you may prove what is the will of God,
what is good and acceptable and perfect.*
—Rom. 12:2 RSV

Even though God reminds us in many ways that we will face trials, we always seem surprised, don't we?

God even tells us that without troubles, we will not be as strong, nor will our faith see the growth we need—growing faith in Him. The point of all this friction is to help us learn to rely on God, not ourselves. We will always be weaker on our own.

How else but through these experiences—the waiting, the wondering, the if and the when of it all—will our faith grow stronger? We learn to hold on to the goodness of God as our lifeline, sometimes simply treading water and trusting to be saved out of the water in His timing!

We know God loves us. This is our hope! We know that God has promised to save us. This is our confidence! We know His ways are trustworthy, so we bend to the trial asking Him to do His work in us through it!

> *Count it all joy, my brethren, when you meet various trials, for you know that the testing of your faith produces steadfastness. And let steadfastness have its full effect, that you may be perfect and complete, lacking in nothing. If any of you lacks wisdom, let him ask God, who gives to all men generously and without reproaching, and it will be given him.*
>
> *—James 1:2–5 RSV*

How are you doing when the trials show up at your door?
Do you run into His arms, or do you run away?

Day Thirty-One

Yesterday is history. Tomorrow is a mystery. Today is a gift.
That's why we call it "The Present."
—Eleanor Roosevelt

Well, one thing, at least, is good: It is for a man to eat well, drink a good
glass of wine, accept his position in life, and enjoy his work whatever his job
may be, for however long the Lord may let him live. And, of course, it is very
good if a man has received wealth from the Lord and the good health to enjoy
it. To enjoy your work and to accept your lot in life—that is indeed a gift
from God. The person who does that will not need to look back with sorrow
on his past, for God gives him joy.
—Eccles. 5:18–20 TLB

We have a tendency to focus on things ahead (or behind) and get distracted from what is going on right around us.

When driving, we can tend to think of arriving and sacrifice the journey! We can get into trouble taking our eyes off the road trying to watch the tragedy on the side of the road. We can even sit in the midst of glorious beauty and be weighed down, so unaware of the gift God has for us right in front of our very eyes!

If we resist the pressure to rush and be distracted by our thoughts, if we can just slow down and enjoy the journey moment by moment, we may realize how thankful and blessed we are!

> *But whatever is good and perfect comes to us from God, the Creator of all light, and he shines forever without change or shadow.*
>
> —James 1:17 TLB

There is so much beauty and grace, so many friends and sweet moments, and gorgeous scenery that we often miss. Let's be aware and grateful to be in this day with our God and each other in this moment!

Look around, friend! What is right around you that you might be missing?

Day Thirty-Two

A poor person isn't he who has little, but he who needs a lot.
—German Proverb

To me, contentment is a sense of balance and peace with ourselves just as we are, no matter the lot we have been given.

Contentment has very little to do with money or things, but more to do with our attitude as we live day to day. Our outlook is greatly affected by where our attention lies, who we put our trust in, and what our expectations are.

O God, I beg two favors from you; let me have them before I die. First, help me never to tell a lie. Second, give me neither poverty nor riches! Give me just enough to satisfy my needs. For if I grow rich, I may deny you and say, "Who is the LORD?" And if I am too poor, I may steal and thus insult God's holy name.
—Prov. 30:7–9

I have noticed and sometimes been led into the temptation that having money to spare actually feeds the stresses of life. That is, although you may still be concerned about mounting bills, you may also experience the distraction and time required to spend that largesse.

It isn't the money itself so much as the constant pull to spend more and more time on it and less and less time being fruitful for God. Certainly, success is a blessing. But it can also be an opportunity to be tested to see where our hearts are. Do we have contentment, or are we busy, distracted, and restless?

> *Don't love money; be satisfied with what you have. For God has said, "I will never fail you. I will never abandon you." So we can say with confidence, "The LORD is my helper, so I will have no fear. What can mere people do to me?"*
>
> —Heb. 13:5–6

> *Yet true godliness with contentment is itself great wealth.*
>
> —1 Tim. 6:6

Do you need to pray for your attitude and focus to change to be more content right now?

Day Thirty-Three

Friendship, of itself a holy tie, is made more sacred by adversity.
—John Dryden

During the good times of life, friendship forges memories and good feelings about all the joys we've experienced together. In fact, it's difficult to deepen a relationship if we never spend time together! It takes effort to begin and effort to keep a good friend. If we've ever experienced any trials or adversity, we find out very quickly who is a true friend!

> *Since God chose you to be the holy people he loves, you must clothe yourselves with tenderhearted mercy, kindness, humility, gentleness, and patience. Make allowance for each other's faults, and forgive anyone who offends you. Remember, the LORD forgave you, so you must forgive others. Above all, clothe yourselves with love, which binds us all together in perfect harmony.*
> —Col. 3:12–14

Do I forgive friends easily? Do I reach out in concern and compassion, patiently helping in sickness, being kind despite my friend's faults, encouraging, and being supportive and concerned for their welfare? Am I there in the celebrations and just as much there when things are difficult for them?

Today, let's examine our capacity to be a friend; let's appreciate and pray for our friends who've been there for us!

Thank you, Father, for placing friends in our lives. Please bless them, watch over them, and heal and help them. Help me to be there when my friends are in need!

> *Two people are better off than one, for they can help each other succeed. If one person falls, the other can reach out and help. But someone who falls alone is in real trouble. Likewise, two people lying close together can keep each other warm. But how can one be warm alone? A person standing alone can be attacked and defeated, but two can stand back-to-back and conquer. Three are even better, for a triple-braided cord is not easily broken.*
> —Eccles. 4:9–12

Is there a friend you need to be there for in a better way than you have?

Day Thirty-Four

To get the full value of joy, you must have someone to divide it with.
—Mark Twain

When my anxious thoughts multiply within me, your comforts delight me.
—Ps. 94:19 AMP

It would be so easy to herald the value of our friendships. It is true, friendships are good for our health and growth throughout life. Sometimes, however, we find ourselves feeling alone. I think you know exactly those moments.

You may have felt all alone when you received news of a sudden death, or you may know that isolating feeling of waiting for a call for test results. Sometimes, we find ourselves in a desperate isolating prayer when most aware of our sin or when we struggle to forgive another, and we carry the hurt alone.

You may feel terribly alone sitting in silence at the bedside of an unconscious loved one, or it's that empty, quiet, dark late night when sleep escapes us, and the heavy weight of something keeps us pacing!

What struck me so much about this direction of my thoughts is the profound truth that I am not alone at all! You are not alone at all!

For in the day of trouble He will hide me in His shelter; in the secret place of His tent He will hide me; He will lift me up on a rock.

—Ps. 27:5 AMP

We are His, and He is ours. We have a champion for our cause, faithful in those moments when no one or anything can get close. He is our quiet joy when there isn't someone to tell—our Savior when nothing else could save us and our sure Hope when hope seems impossible to believe in!

God is a secure anchor, a solid foundation, a strong cornerstone, and a sure tower of strength for us!

You have given me greater joy than those who have abundant harvests of grain and new wine. In peace I will lie down and sleep, for you alone, O Lord, will keep me safe.

—Ps. 4:7–8

Can you recall when your God has been the only one you could turn to?

Day Thirty-Five

I have not failed. I've just found 10,000 ways that don't work.
—Thomas Edison

This is my command—be strong and courageous! Do not be afraid or discouraged. For the LORD your God is with you wherever you go.
—Josh. 1:9

I love the tenacity of our famous inventor Thomas Edison. Oh, he wasn't understood at all during his youth! He was relegated to be homeschooled by the only one who believed in him, his mother, because his teachers thought him "unteachable."

I'm sure, like many inventors, he was just chock-full of thoughts and seemed to be dreaming rather than cooperating. But look what the fruit of all his genius brought to our world—light and musical sound and so many improvements to make our lives more efficient!

How often do we dismiss people because we don't "get" them? They are different, don't fit in, or seem uniquely odd to us? Maybe, just maybe, they are exactly as God designed them to be!

> *But as for you, be strong and courageous, for your work will be rewarded.*
> —2 Chron. 15:7

Perhaps we seem strange to other people, trying to be a Christian in this world. Maybe we are a little odd to others, living with our desire to please the God who shaped us rather than pleasing man!

> *Don't be afraid, for I am with you. Don't be discouraged, for I am your God.*
> *I will strengthen you and help you. I will hold you up with my victorious*
> *right hand.*
> —Isa. 41:10

We can live with the same tenacity that Edison had in his work. We can keep striving for excellence. We can keep our lives pleasing to God even if we seem a bit odd to others we meet!

> *For I can do everything through Christ, who gives me strength.*
> —Phil. 4:13

Have you tried to live for God but found the world pulling at you still?

Day Thirty-Six

To be a Christian without prayer is no more possible than
to be alive without breathing.
—Martin Luther

Lord All-Powerful, you test good people. You look deeply into a person's mind.
—Jer. 20:12 ERV

What if prayer could be so much more than checking in with God each day, so much deeper than presenting my list of needs and desires? What if prayer could be so essential to me that it would be as natural and as necessary as breathing?

What if I can really get so close to the feet of my Savior and be so able to connect with Him each morning, each moment, that prayer would be as necessary to me as my breath is to my life? Well, I can!

It can all begin with saving my first waking moments to think of Him. I can arise from my bed and channel my first energies toward running to be with Him, rather than running around, running off the rails, running into trouble, and running into arguments.

If I could see prayer as a " lifeline" for the day and a "life preserver" to a soul who may be over her head in a vast sea of weighty circumstances, then I could catch those first morning breaths to talk with my God, sing out to Him, and just breathe!

And when we are so under the gun, over our heads, or beneath a load too heavy to bear or even speak of, God's Holy Spirit breathes for us:

> *Also, the Spirit helps us. We are very weak, but the Spirit helps us with our weakness. We don't know how to pray as we should, but the Spirit himself speaks to God for us. He begs God for us, speaking to him with feelings too deep for words. God already knows our deepest thoughts. And he understands what the Spirit is saying, because the Spirit speaks for his people in the way that agrees with what God wants.*
>
> —Rom. 8:26–27 ERV

> *God, the one and only—I'll wait as long as he says. Everything I hope for comes from him, so why not? He's solid rock under my feet, breathing room for my soul.*
>
> —Ps. 62:5–6 MSG

Can you take a deep breath in and feel life entering into your very being?
Now release a long slow breath out, leaving the peace that God wants for you today!

Day Thirty-Seven

The greatest good you can do for another is not just to share your riches, but to reveal to him his own.

—Benjamin Disraeli

"For I know the plans I have for you," says the LORD. "They are plans for good and not for disaster, to give you a future and a hope."

—Jer. 29:11

Was there someone in your life who saw the hidden potential in you? I am sure that you can recall very clearly anyone who complimented you and built you up when you were a child or teen. And I'm doubly sure that you can recall the discouraging words that anyone ever said even more clearly.

We all have talent. Some is still hidden potential in us because, over the years, those discouraging words can steal our confidence. We all need those sweet voices to remind us of who we really are!

On our own, we often whisper negative and critical words into our own hearts. Maybe those are the past memories of hurtful words. We need people in our lives who can see through the shyness or reserve, down to the depths of who we can be! We need people who are better than we often are to ourselves.

Then we need to pass on that same kindness. We can seek to be one of those positive voices for another. Who do you see raw talent in—talent that may not fully be developed yet? This may be someone who just needs a positive push to get them off their mark.

What a blessing to be that for someone!

What a blessing to have someone be that for you!

What a privilege to be called by God to help guide someone along!

> *Now all glory to God, who is able, through his mighty power at work within us, to accomplish infinitely more than we might ask or think.*
>
> —Eph. 3:20

> *For we are God's masterpiece. He has created us anew in Christ Jesus, so we can do the good things he planned for us long ago.*
>
> —Eph. 2:10

Ask God to inspire you to notice the hidden potential in someone you can encourage.

Day Thirty-Eight

A bit of fragrance clings to the hand that gives flowers.
—Chinese Proverb

*Oil and perfume make the heart glad, and the sweetness of
a friend comes from his earnest counsel.*
—Prov. 27:9 ESV

Have you ever thought of yourself as being either a fragrant experience for someone or, sadly, an unpleasant memory?

When you walk away from someone, is it as if a lovely aroma has just passed through, leaving a pleasant sensation trailing behind? Have you thought how your words can be sweet, uplifting, even life-giving and encouraging, or how your careless words can create a wasted, shallow experience?

Our lives are a Christ-like fragrance rising up to God.

—2 Cor. 2:15

We can be a sweet message of life and inspiration, offering hope and help if we take the time to be intentional. If we guard our tongues and are careful, we can intentionally spread a sweet fragrance around to others! And this will always be rewarded with a lingering joy left behind and a happy heart aware of and pleasing to our God!

> *Live a life filled with love, following the example of Christ. He loved us and offered himself as a sacrifice for us, a pleasing aroma to God.*
>
> —Eph. 5:2

> *And do everything with love.*
>
> —1 Cor. 16:14

Looking back, have your words and behavior been a sweet fragrance to those around you?

Day Thirty-Nine

To make your children capable of honesty is the beginning of education.
—John Ruskin

*The path of integrity is always safe, but a person who follows a
crooked way will be exposed.*
—Prov. 10:9 VOICE

We might have chuckled to each other when a three-year-old with chocolate crumbs on his mouth says, "No, I didn't take that cookie." However, all of us know that it's necessary to watch out for the signs of deception in our children. We want to know we can trust them as they trust us, right?

It's part of our teaching to guide them on integrity so they can be good citizens and add morality to their world. Obviously, our world shows many signs of bad or no parenting by the number of prisons. It starts in the home, doesn't it?

I remember the first time early in our marriage when my husband asked me if I had done something that I was supposed to do for us. I had failed to follow through. I remember struggling at that moment about whether to tell him the truth: Should I admit it, or not? I decided in that moment that I would not start off our marriage lying to him! I told him the truth. The truth wasn't so hard, and the result was even better—the beginning of an honest and trusting relationship for us both!

> *Honesty guides good people; dishonesty destroys treacherous people.*
>
> —Prov. 11:3

Honesty in all our relationships is so important. Honesty with God is paramount! Funny thing is, God already knows the truth!

> *An honest answer is like a kiss of friendship.*
>
> —Prov. 24:26

> *The LORD is more pleased when we do what is right and just than when we offer him sacrifices.*
>
> —Prov. 21:3

Have you been honest in your relationships with others and with your God?

Day Forty

The greatest virtues are those which are most useful to other persons.

— Aristotle

God has given each of you a gift from his great variety of spiritual gifts.
Use them well to serve one another.

—1 Pet. 4:10

I'm so glad that we women are all uniquely different. God has made us that way! Interdependence causes us to need each other's abilities. It helps us be amazed at others' talents. We appreciate and validate each other because we see something God-given in every precious life!

It's all right if I lack your gift. Wouldn't the world be a strange place if we were all just alike? There would be unmet needs everywhere! Because we all hold back,

I'm afraid there still are unmet needs. We often feel isolated, shy, selfish, or self-promoting, and the joy of giving ourselves away isn't practiced nearly enough!

What can we women do to help fix this problem? First of all, we can recognize and appreciate our own ability. Thank God for your unique giftedness! Now, ask yourself, "Am I using my gift only for myself?" We can ask God to show us someone who needs us. We can do it!

Let's take a baby step today to use that gift for someone else! Life will be so much more exciting and rewarding when we do!

> *Work willingly at whatever you do, as though you were working for the Lord rather than for people. Remember that the Lord will give you an inheritance as your reward, and that the Master you are serving is Christ.*
> —Col. 3:23–24

> *The master said, "Well done, my good and faithful servant."*
> —Matt. 25:23

What gift has God blessed you with, and how can you be of help to someone today?

Day Forty-One

People need dreams, there's as much nourishment in them as food.
—Dorothy Gilman

Commit your actions to the Lord, and your plans will succeed.
—Prov. 16:3

Do you have a dream? It's good to dream! Do you wish in vain for something impossible to happen? It can!

Are we afraid to dream, to want for better, to wish for good things to change another or ourselves? Sometimes, dreaming big can lead us to make needed changes that move us closer to what we most want.

Change starts with a dream, and if we turn the dream into a fervent prayer and keep seeking God, He will guide our dreams and help us achieve what yesterday seemed unattainable!

Sometimes, He may work on our minds through our prayers to alter our perceptions about our dreams, possibly tweaking them into something even better than we could imagine happening!

So, don't be afraid to dream big, and don't be afraid to voice your dreams to your dear Father who wants the best for each of His children! His strength, added to our desire, may just be the strong cord that will pull our dreams forward into reality!

> *But you, who are devoted to being with God and searching for God, be strong and do not lose courage because your actions will reap rewards.*
> —2 Chron. 15:7 VOICE

> *For I'm going to do a brand-new thing. See, I have already begun! Don't you see it? I will make a road through the wilderness of the world for my people to go home, and create rivers for them in the desert!*
> —Isa. 43:19 TLB

> *Ask, and you will be given what you ask for. Seek, and you will find. Knock, and the door will be opened. For everyone who asks, receives. Anyone who seeks, finds. If only you will knock, the door will open.*
> —Matt. 7:7–8 TLB

Is there a dream you haven't dared to put into words yet? Ask Him!

Day Forty-Two

Pray to God, but row away from the rocks.
—Hunter S. Thompson

Run from anything that stimulates youthful lusts. Instead, pursue righteous living, faithfulness, love, and peace. Enjoy the companionship of those who call on the Lord with pure hearts.
—2 Tim. 2:22

We can cry out to God at any moment, and He wants us to bring Him into every situation we have. For He can transform, He can provide the lifeboat, He can comfort, and He can help us resist.

But there is our part too, as women! We must recognize the tempting places, the weakest parts of ourselves, and run from the rocks that are ready to swamp our lifeboat! Today, let's examine ourselves:

How much am I tempted because of my own choices?

Do I ever call on the Lord in these moments, or do I attempt the rescue alone?

Do I teeter on the fine line between good and evil?

Do I surround myself with friends who can pull me up, or do they drag me down?

Let's examine ourselves and if we have foundered on the rocks, there is a way back to safety. Ask and have your heart cleansed with His healing balm of forgiveness!

O Lord, you are so good, so ready to forgive, so full of unfailing love for all who ask for your help. Listen closely to my prayer, O LORD; hear my urgent cry. I will call to you whenever I'm in trouble, and you will answer me.

—Ps. 86:5–7

When you are in trouble, call for Me. I will come and rescue you, and you will honor Me.

—Ps. 50:15 VOICE

Can you truly be honest with God today about your temptations?

Day Forty-Three

Every tomorrow has two handles. We can take hold of it with the handle of anxiety or the handle of faith.
—Henry Ward Beecher

But when I am afraid, I will put my confidence in you. Yes, I will trust the promises of God. And since I am trusting him, what can mere man do to me?
—Ps. 56:3–4 TLB

Faith or Anxiety: Which do I feed? Which do I nourish?

Anxiety is really fear turned on ourselves. When I'm afraid or feeling a bit insecure—maybe choices need to be made, decisions need to be exercised, or hard things walked through—my fears can lead to an anxious mind, sleepless nights,

and worrying thoughts. When that happens, I can become forgetful. I forget God's wonderful caring, His promises of protection, and His tools for equipping me.

Instead of focusing on all those good things, I become focused on my inadequacies and my lack of provision and ability. I begin to feed the anxiety by giving it more time and more attention. Prayer is often forgotten and so is my ability to ask for help from my God during these times.

Faith takes courage! Faith is the opposite of fear. I'm talking about the faith to remember to trust God, not myself! That's the key! Our God has big shoulders to bear our burdens!

> *When doubts filled my mind, your comfort gave me renewed hope and cheer.*
> —Ps. 94:19

> *For God has not given us a spirit of fear and timidity, but of power, love, and self-discipline.*
> —2 Tim. 1:7

Has there been an opportunity lately for you to choose faith over anxiety?

Day Forty-Four

The art of being wise is the art of knowing what to overlook.
—William James

A person's wisdom yields patience; it is to one's glory to overlook an offense.
—Prov. 19:11 NIV

We've all been there: saying just a little more than we should, acting a bit nutty and later wondering what someone must think of us?

We might go back and mention our behavior or even ask forgiveness for our thoughtlessness only to find that the other person hasn't taken offense, or they generously give us the benefit of the doubt.

We can't believe that others could accept us—that they actually like us just as we are! Imagine that! What a beautiful, artful thing in this world—that we can be accepted for who we are! We all need this generosity and, sometimes, forgiveness.

We all crave this too—the ability to be ourselves, warts and all, and still be loved! It's a very noble and generous trait to let others be themselves and be generous toward them in their quirky ways.

That's really all of us! We all need the open arms of acceptance for who we are down deep. I pray today we can be that for each other and appreciate each other as we really are!

Above all, love each other deeply, because love covers over a multitude of sins.
—1 Pet. 4:8 NIV

Are you able to be yourself and let others be themselves?

Day Forty-Five

When you arise in the morning, think of what a precious privilege it is to be alive—to breathe, to think, to enjoy, to love.

—Marcus Aurelius

Even so, I have noticed one thing, at least, that is good. It is good for people to eat, drink, and enjoy their work under the sun during the short life God has given them, and to accept their lot in life. And it is a good thing to receive wealth from God and the good health to enjoy it. To enjoy your work and accept your lot in life—this is indeed a gift from God. God keeps such people so busy enjoying life that they take no time to brood over the past.

—Eccles. 5:18–20

What is true wealth? Isn't it to recognize and appreciate just how blessed we are right now in this moment of our lives? We look around and have the spiritual eyes to see how fortunate our lot in life really is.

We can take for granted that we have a solid roof over our heads, people in our lives to care about, food enough so that we never go hungry, work to do to earn our way, family ties that connect us deeply to life, miraculous things occurring right in our backyard, and a God who cherishes us from creation to eternal reward!

Let's count our many blessings. Let's be grateful today for our loved ones and celebrate the loving relationships that are all around us!

Open for me the gates where the righteous enter, and I will go in and thank the Lord. *This is the day the* Lord *has made. We will rejoice and be glad in it.*
— Ps.118:19, 24

Can you ask God today to open your eyes to see clearly all your blessings?

Day Forty-Six

A faith is a necessity to a man. Woe to him who believes in nothing.
—Victor Hugo

*I remember your genuine faith, for you share the faith that
first filled your grandmother Lois and your mother, Eunice.
And I know that same faith continues strong in you.
This is why I remind you to fan into flames the spiritual
gift God gave you when I laid my hands on you.
For God has not given us a spirit of fear and timidity,
but of power, love, and self-discipline.*

—2 Tim. 1:5–7

Everyone is a person of faith. Even atheists have a religion—one in which the god of self sits on the throne of their lives. The kind of faith God asks of us is a seed of trust placed in Him. Just a small move in the direction of trusting God over self can germinate and thrive and become a true and lasting relationship that never ends, saved in heaven, for those who take the journey!

Faith begins with a realization of how powerless we are and how little strength we have alone. It continues to grow as we ask God to come into our lives, understanding the impossible nature of our sin condition. No matter how many good works we do, we can't wash away the sin problem we have.

When we desire to turn away from the old life of sin and finally understand the tremendous sacrifice Christ made on the cross for us, then faith can do its transforming work. I want my faith to be genuine and strong!

> *The apostles said to the Lord, "Show us how to increase our faith." The Lord answered, "If you had faith even as small as a mustard seed, you could say to this mulberry tree, 'May you be uprooted and be planted in the sea,' and it would obey you!"*
>
> —Luke 17:5–6

Can you pray to see that small beginning of faith flowering into a genuine and beautiful relationship with Christ?

Day Forty-Seven

The greatest sweetener of human life is friendship.
—Joseph Addison

A friend loves at all times, and a brother is born for adversity.
—Prov. 17:17 RSV

Many people walk around deprived of the delicious dessert of friends. I had my family of sisters and brother; later I had my husband and daughters, but outside of those sweet relationships, I had never trusted enough to risk opening my heart to a girlfriend.

I must admit that I had a really good friend in high school, and we were like what most young girls are as friends, inseparable. But she moved away and left me all alone to finish school that last year. I drifted. My response was, "Never again!"

It seems so silly now that I would actually have been angry at her when it was her parents' job change that was at fault. It's only in recent years that God has opened me up to trusting and hoping and wanting sweet friendships.

Anger, fear, and trust issues can keep us from many rich and wonderful moments. We live a dry, less-enhanced existence without the joy, the growth, and the wonderful opportunity to be gifted with friends.

Ask God today to help you see that right around you are people who could be your friends—someone who could sweeten your life as friends have enriched mine!

You use steel to sharpen steel, and one friend sharpens another.
—Prov. 27:17 MSG

Is friendship-making difficult for you?
Can you ask God for courage to open your eyes and see someone He might be placing in your path who could become a sweet friend to you?

Day Forty-Eight

Anger makes you smaller, while forgiveness forces you to grow beyond what you were.
—Chérie Carter-Scott

Understand this, my dear brothers and sisters: You must all be quick to listen, slow to speak, and slow to get angry. Human anger does not produce the righteousness God desires.
—James 1:19–20

A nger is an inevitable response to living together. Where two or more are gathered, there will be times of anger.

In marriages, things get said that hurt. In families, brothers and sisters irritate and rub each other wrong. In traffic, rudeness and inattention can raise the ire quickly! In neighborhoods, churches, and government, there are opportunities for anger to occur.

Sometimes, it's righteous anger against injustice, unfairness, or stupidity that gets our dander up! But no matter what causes our feelings, God asks us to deal with them by forgiving. Even if it requires a constant return to forgiveness, we must do it.

> *Then Peter came to him and asked, "Lord, how often should I forgive someone who sins against me? Seven times?" "No, not seven times," Jesus replied, "but seventy times seven!"*
>
> —Matt. 18:21–22

Why such a difficult standard? Why such a hard challenge?

> *Get rid of all bitterness, rage, anger, harsh words, and slander, as well as all types of evil behavior. Instead, be kind to each other, tenderhearted, forgiving one another, just as God through Christ has forgiven you.*
>
> —Eph. 4:31–32

Yes, much is required because we have been forgiven everything! Yes, it's a great challenge! Yes, forgiveness requires a great deal of prayer to accomplish. But it's life-giving to us when we do.

> *He who is slow to anger is better and more honorable than the mighty [soldier], and he who rules and controls his own spirit, than he who captures a city.*
>
> —Prov. 16:32 AMP

Anyone you need to forgive today?
Anyone you need to seek forgiveness from today?

Day Forty-Nine

Expectation is the root of all heartache.
—William Shakespeare

Hope deferred makes the heart sick, but a longing fulfilled is a tree of life.
—Prov. 13:12 NIV

We watch the first soft pink colors in the eastern sky, and we expect a beautiful sunrise to follow.

We have high expectations of our marriages, of our children, of our friends, of our leaders, of the seasons, of the day, and of our future. Sometimes, we are unrealistic and get our hopes up, only to become discouraged!

Sometimes, we are just plain illogical or confused, and we really can get disappointed when things don't happen as we expect. I have seen marriages fall apart because of a wife or husband expecting perfection in their spouse!

Children may become exasperated at a parent who pushes them into a dream that isn't theirs and a path that doesn't fit them all because a mom or dad thinks that is best for their child!

Friendships are hurt and churches divide over unmet expectations. Governments topple, and leaders are unseated because of unfulfilled promises!

> *Yes, my soul, find rest in God; my hope comes from him. Truly he is my rock and my salvation; he is my fortress, I will not be shaken. My salvation and my honor depend on God; he is my mighty rock, my refuge. Trust in him at all times, you people; pour out your hearts to him, for God is our refuge.*
> —Ps. 62:5–8 NIV

Look to God and have high expectations. But when it comes to human beings, grace has to be the watchword, or we will always expect too much and find ourselves disappointed.

We ourselves are flawed. We get our hopes up too high. We get hurt, or we fail each other at times. Only God will always be there, always be faithful and true, always be consistent, and always keep His promises. Today, let's put our faith and trust in God and be gracious to everyone else.

> *Trust in the LORD with all your heart and lean not on your own understanding; in all your ways submit to him, and he will make your paths straight.*
> —Prov. 3:5–6 NIV

Have you expected too much from someone you love?

Day Fifty

*Love doesn't sit there like a stone; it has to be made, like bread;
remade all the time, made new.*
—Ursula K. Le Guin

*And so we know and rely on the love God has for us. God is love.
Whoever lives in love lives in God, and God in them. This is how love is made
complete among us so that we will have confidence on the day of judgment:
In this world we are like Jesus.*
—1 John 4:16–17 NIV

There is something so intoxicating about the smell of bread baking. The wafting scent will permeate the whole house and curl out of the doors into the open air or draw you into a bakery with its aroma.

Bread doesn't last long. If it's good, it's consumed quickly, or if it sits unused, it begins to mold and go bad. In fact, before bread was packaged and preserved and sold commercially, it was a daily production in homes, and the day began with making bread for a hungry family. Bread, called the staff of life, is the energy that fuels the body—the source of comfort and the completion to a good meal.

Love is like that! We don't tell our spouse or child that we love them one time and then never again. No, we say it every day and display it throughout our lives by our actions toward them. Love needs to be refreshed and grow and alive just like the active yeast found in bread.

Who do you love? Who do I love? Jesus asks us to let our love grow to include everyone—even our enemies! Recently someone remarked to me that rather than trying to change others, we should just love them and let God do the changing! I like that!

We seek God because He is love. He teaches us how to love, and then we can be complete and confident people!

And hope does not put us to shame, because God's love has been poured out into our hearts through the Holy Spirit, who has been given to us.
—Rom. 5:5 NIV

How can you pour yourself out in love today?

Day Fifty-One

The best way to cheer yourself up is to try to cheer somebody else up.
—Mark Twain

Therefore encourage and comfort one another and build up one another,
just as you are doing.
—1 Thess. 5:11 AMP

I don't know exactly how it works, but I do know without a doubt that it does work! This seemingly conflicting idea is true: I can feel better myself by taking my mind off myself and focusing on another's needs. Amazingly, my own countenance will be transformed.

If I'm weighed down by fear or worry and I focus my mind on loving another by turning to prayer for their concerns, then my own fears and worries fade away without being fed!

It's one of those admonitions given to us by a God who knows us better than we know ourselves! He knows that when I want to crawl into a corner and stew, what I need most is to crawl out into the light and tend to the needs of others.

> *I pray that God, the source of hope, will fill you completely with joy and peace because you trust in him. Then you will overflow with confident hope through the power of the Holy Spirit.*
>
> —Rom. 15:13

I will overflow with joy and peace and I will be lifted up when I focus not on me! We can soar beyond our limited understanding to high places where fish and loaves are multiplied, hearts are healed, lives are helped, laps are overflowing, needs are met, and futures are changed—all because we heed the admonition to love others!

> *Give, and it will be given to you. A good measure, pressed down, shaken together and running over, will be poured into your lap. For with the measure you use, it will be measured to you.*
>
> —Luke 6:38 NIV

When fear or worry come calling, who can you call on in love?

Day Fifty-Two

Love looks through a telescope;
envy through a microscope.
—Josh Billings

Wrath is cruel, anger is overwhelming,
but who can stand before jealousy?
—Prov. 27:4 ESV

Have you fallen into the trap of comparison? We desire to have what others have; we covet their house or their spouse, their skin, or their kin!

We see ourselves as less, and we dwell on the inequities of life, and we covet instead of care; we resent instead of living sent!

Where there is jealousy and selfishness, there will be confusion and every kind of evil.

—James 3:16 ERV

So, if we notice that we tend to wish and want and envy and feel left out of life, we can ask God to help us change that attitude. Instead of envying, why don't we choose to admire, encourage, and be happy for what others have. We could notice and compliment those around us. We could choose to be excited for the richness of their lives!

The by-product of this change in thinking will be a newfound joy in who we are! We will become kind, loving, and contented people who will be appreciated by others. We will be rich in love and good works. We will be overflowing with a bounty far better than anything we can lust after!

Delight yourself in the LORD, and he will give you the desires of your heart.
—Ps. 37:4 ESV

Have you had difficulty being happy for other people who seem more blessed than you?
Can you pause and remember all the blessings that God has given you?

Day Fifty-Three

Each day is a little life; every waking and rising a little birth; every morning a little youth; every going to rest and sleep a little death.
—Arthur Schopenhauer

So teach us to number our days that we may get a heart of wisdom.
—Ps. 90:12 ESV

What a very profound idea—to live each day fully as though it was our only day. In our first waking moments, we'd arise to an excitement and awareness of beauty, possibility, and expectancy for our day. We'd think about all that we love and care about. Our hearts would turn first to our God, grateful for this life, this place, this day, and those we love.

We'd lift up to Him every need of those who need us, aware of all that was most important. We'd not want to waste a moment, would we? We'd want to do what was most important in that day.

During that day, each interaction with anyone would be deemed precious, knowing that this would be our only day, wouldn't it? We'd want to say what was most important to each one, and we wouldn't want wasted motion to tick away the precious hours, would we?

We'd make sure we didn't hurt any relationship on that one day! And when that day was over and we laid our heads on our pillows, we'd examine our minds and our day and then clear our consciences of anything that might separate us from our God, wouldn't we?

It is challenging to think about approaching each day as our one day to live! How would that one day be for me, for you?

> *"So don't be anxious about tomorrow. God will take care of your tomorrow too. Live one day at a time."*
>
> —Matt. 6:34 TLB

> *For I know the plans I have for you, says the LORD. They are plans for good and not for evil, to give you a future and a hope.*
>
> —Jer. 29:11 TLB

Has it been a challenge for you to live one day at a time?

Day Fifty-Four

What great thing would you attempt if you knew you could not fail?
—Robert H. Schuller

*"This is my command—be strong and courageous! Do not be afraid or discouraged. For the L*ORD *your God is with you wherever you go."*
—Josh. 1:9 NLT

Is there something that you would do, create, attempt, begin, get back to, unearth, or finish if you knew that you could not fail at it?

Thinking this way opens up some deep desires, doesn't it? It also points out for me how alone I feel when I begin to think about attempting anything! I lack confidence in myself. I hear that discouraging voice that dooms me before I even begin.

It's that negative self-talk—that absence of an encouraging voice urging me forward. Those are the reasons I can talk myself right out of believing in myself.

But then I tell myself that God is that supernatural, miraculous power and element that I forgot to include in my thinking! This knowledge helps me begin to believe that maybe, just maybe, with His strength in me, His wings under me, His voice surrounding me and urging me on, I can do what I thought I couldn't do, or what I thought would fail if I attempted it!

First, I know this:

> *You formed the way I think and feel. You put me together in my mother's womb. I praise you because you made me in such a wonderful way. I know how amazing that was!*
>
> —Ps. 139:13–14 ERV

And then I know this:

> *But those who trust in the LORD will be blessed. They know that the LORD will do what he says. They will be strong like trees planted near a stream that send out roots to the water. They have nothing to fear when the days get hot. Their leaves are always green. They never worry, even in a year that has no rain. They always produce fruit.*
>
> —Jer. 17:7–8 ERV

Does knowing all this give you courage, as it does me, to attempt something new?

Day Fifty-Five

A book holds a house of gold.
—Chinese Proverb

I will study your instructions. I will give thought to your way of life.
—Ps. 119:15 ERV

We were given a pretty little book as a wedding gift. I tucked it into our bookshelf. Years went by, and one day I finally looked at it.

During all those years of our marriage, we went about making adjustments, coping with having and raising children, handling struggles with discipline and teaching, living, and making lots of life choices. All that time, I had no idea of the wealth of advice and counsel that was tucked into those pages!

How can a young person live a pure life? By obeying your word. I try with all my heart to serve you. Help me obey your commands.

—Ps. 119:9–10 ERV

I was without some much-needed wisdom! Right there close and within reach was a lifeline that I never grabbed. On every subject, that little book contained the path to good communication, decision-making, love, joy, peace—all the wealth of advice a married person could use! It's the same with another little book—the Bible.

This book too often sits on shelves, untouched. This too is a lifeline within easy reach. It contains a treasure of wisdom, solutions, comfort, counsel, and assurances. The Bible is the pathway to life!

Great blessings belong to those who follow his rules! They seek him with all their heart.

—Ps. 119:2 ERV

Have you discovered and mined the rich wealth of wisdom and help found in His Word?

Day Fifty-Six

The closing years of life are like the end of a masquerade party,
when the masks are dropped.
—Arthur Schopenhauer

But the Lord said, "My grace is all you need. Only when you are weak can
everything be done completely by my power." So I will gladly boast about my
weaknesses. Then Christ's power can stay in me.
—2 Cor. 12:9 ERV

It takes a great deal of our own energy to keep a mask on. Keeping up appearances and avoiding deep revealing conversations that expose us to another can be a lonely place to dwell.

Oh, sure, someone may be amazed at you, thinking you have no failings or flaws or problems or weaknesses, but being yourself is what can draw someone to you. It's the shared challenges, the insecurities, the struggles, the common burdens of our natures that make us approachable and real. If you are feeling a bit lonely, ask yourself, "Am I wearing a mask to keep people from really knowing who I am down deep?"

Sometimes, even marriages can be lonely places if two people aren't willing to open up completely. We might feel that we aren't loved for ourselves if we aren't allowing our true selves to be loved!

The secret is that God can be our strength as we allow our weaknesses to show. Our weaknesses are there, but they don't have to define us. They can help us to grow stronger as we see our needs and seek our strength by trusting in God.

Christ is the one who gives me the strength I need to do whatever I must do.
—Phil. 4:13 ERV

Do you know God thinks you are wonderful just the way you are?

Day Fifty-Seven

Character is a diamond that scratches every other stone.
—Cyrus A. Bartol

*Because you have these blessings, do all you can to add to your life these things:
to your faith add goodness; to your goodness add knowledge; to your knowledge
add self-control; to your self-control add patience; to your patience add devotion
to God; to your devotion add kindness toward your brothers and sisters in
Christ, and to this kindness add love.*
—2 Pet. 1:5–7 ERV

The diamond is one of the most sought-after stones. It is a great symbol for marriage, able to withstand whatever life throws at it, not crumbling in the rough and tumble of life's grinding mill.

It took a long time for pressures in the earth to produce a vein of this precious gem! What a great symbol for our commitment to each other!

Our characters are very precious too. We want to develop good character as women. A good character doesn't happen overnight! Like the diamond, it needs the shaping of time and testing. Just like the diamond, good character is shaped by the pressures of life.

Many, many small decisions are made every day. Will we take the high road instead of the easy path? Do we seek a moral code that pleases God, or are we swayed by man's whims? Do we guard our hearts when temptation comes? When we are wrong, do we admit fault and ask forgiveness in humility?

Character is formed in the quiet moments of no one knowing, the way we treat the vulnerable, and the choices we make in heated times. It is honed and chiseled out of the small moments and the pressure cooker of big choices to which we are exposed in our daily lives!

Each day, we can shine the light of God's scrutiny on our character. We can ask Him to show us where we need to grow.

> *Now, young woman, don't be afraid. I will do what you ask. All the people in our town know that you are a very good woman.*
>
> —Ruth 3:11 ERV

What would someone say about your character today?

Day Fifty-Eight

Rough waters are truer tests of leadership.
In calm water every ship has a good captain.
—Swedish Proverb

I know, LORD, that our lives are not our own. We are not able to plan our own
course. So correct me, LORD, but please be gentle.
—Jer. 10:23–24

One value of difficult times is to find out whether we are guiding our own course or allowing God to be our captain.

On smooth sailing days, the wind is perfect. It's so easy to use our own knowledge to guide the boat. The waters are quiet, the wind is a whisper, and the day is lovely. On those days, we can become forgetful. We forget that the days aren't all like that.

What about the stormy days when we're out in the middle of the deep? What about the unexpected squall that hits our tiny ship? In those rough waters, we quickly realize that our strength is not enough!

Oh, to be guided all the time with the gentle nudges of correction, the wisdom to stay on the true course, the gentler ride, and the peace of knowing God is with us at the helm. There is rest for our souls as we depend on Him rather than the loneliness of our own stubborn nature.

> *Yet I still belong to you; you hold my right hand. You guide me with your counsel, leading me to a glorious destiny. Whom have I in heaven but you? I desire you more than anything on earth. My health may fail, and my spirit may grow weak, but God remains the strength of my heart; he is mine forever.*
>
> —Ps. 73:23–26

Have you allowed God to take the lead in your life? Is He your Captain?

Day Fifty-Nine

The virtue lies in the struggle, not in the prize.
—Richard Monckton Milnes

*Three different times I begged the Lord to take it away. Each time he said,
"My grace is all you need. My power works best in weakness."*
—2 Cor. 12:8–9

Doesn't it seem like a contradiction to say that weakness is strength? It seems to go against the grain to admit that we may need the help of the Almighty God! God even instructs us to be strong and not to fear.

But interestingly, the way through is actually to admit we are afraid and to place our confident trust in the One who is able. God is willing, and He is strong enough. For all along, it is God who has the power to handle things for us.

The LORD is a shelter for the oppressed, a refuge in times of trouble. Those who know your name trust in you, for you, O LORD, do not abandon those who search for you.

—Ps. 9:9–10

So, in the end, our very weakness becomes our most powerful tool!

But blessed are those who trust in the LORD and have made the LORD their hope and confidence. They are like trees planted along a riverbank, with roots that reach deep into the water. Such trees are not bothered by the heat or worried by long months of drought. Their leaves stay green, and they never stop producing fruit.

—Jer. 17:7–8

Let's put our roots down deep into the soil of God's heart. Let's draw strength for our marriages, our health challenges, our children, our friendships, and our loved ones' concerns.

Can you see how important it is to admit your weaknesses so that, by depending on God, you are really at your strongest?

Day Sixty

Now on the last and most important day of the feast, Jesus stood and called out [in a loud voice], "If anyone is thirsty, let him come to Me and drink!"
—John 7:37 AMP

Have you ever felt severely parched and been unable to get your thirst quenched? On a trip to Arizona, we went bike riding, but I was unprepared for the arid dryness. By the time we finished our ride, I was extremely parched and felt faint. I had no idea just how depleted of fluids my body was. I could not get enough water!

In this day of water bottles and convenience stores and faucets and rest stops in America, we hardly get to experience dehydration.

I can't imagine how life-threatening it was in the past for those traveling across the world's plains or deserts who were forced to carry their water with them, find a stream or oasis, or perish if caught without!

I wonder if, in God's economy, we are all traveling around parched and dry without fueling ourselves daily, hourly, continuously with the living water that will keep us from ever being parched again?

> *But whoever drinks the water that I give him will never be thirsty again. But the water that I give him will become in him a spring of water [satisfying his thirst for God] welling up [continually flowing, bubbling within him] to eternal life.*
>
> —John 4:14 AMP

May we drink from the well of God and His Word. This is an overflowing fountain that provides the life-giving nourishment to carry us through into our eternal lives with Him!

> *The Spirit and the bride say, "Come!" Everyone who hears this should also say, "Come!" All who are thirsty may come; they can have the water of life as a free gift if they want it.*
>
> —Rev. 22:17 ERV

Are you thirsty today for more of God's living water?

Day Sixty-One

And in the act of making things, just by living their daily lives,
they also make history.
—Anne Bartlett

"Knit us together." I heard the words prayed over us.

Can you picture with me the interweaving of our lives in God's beautiful tapestry? We, as women, only get to gaze at the jumble of the underside of this work of art. We wonder how our thread fits into God's design.

A confusion of knots and hanging strands is visible, and seemingly discordant patterns and colors are displayed on this side of life. We ponder questions such as *why* and *when* and *what* in our limited understanding. God asks us to trust Him in the unanswered queries of our lives.

He makes the whole body fit together perfectly. As each part does its own special work, it helps the other parts grow, so that the whole body is healthy and growing and full of love.

—Eph. 4:16

If we could only get the vantage point of heaven. If we could only see what God sees, how He is involved, and how He knits us all together.

If we could see the front side of the tapestry, we'd see a beautiful woven carpet of artistic perfection that God alone understands. We all are interconnected, all necessary, and all just the perfect lights and darks and tones and shades needed to bring the pattern to life.

Next time you feel alone or unnecessary, remember how important you are to God's design in this beautiful work of art. Someday, we'll get to see the front side of the tapestry. Someday, we'll be given the gift of understanding of how we all fit together!

Until then . . .

You made all the delicate, inner parts of my body and knit me together in my mother's womb. Thank you for making me so wonderfully complex! Your workmanship is marvelous—how well I know it.

—Ps. 139:13–14

Have you ever wondered how you fit into God's beautiful design?

Day Sixty-Two

It is only with the heart that one can see rightly;
what is essential is invisible to the eye.
—Antoine de Saint-Exupéry

For now we see in a mirror dimly, but then face to face. Now I know in part;
then I shall know fully, even as I have been fully known.
—1 Cor. 13:12 ESV

The mirrors spoken of in ancient times were not like our mirrors today. We get an actual visual of every blemish and pore with our mirrors. Not so then. The best they could hope for was a polished metal tray or a reflective pool of water in which to see their faces.

Did they better understand then that just as their image was dim, so too was their ability to see themselves honestly or see what part God played in their lives?

I wish our spiritual vision could be as sharp as our mirrors are today! We often justify sinful choices because our spiritual vision is blurred. We often fail to trust God when He requires certain things of us, or we question why He warns us of behaviors and lifestyles that may harm us!

We try to use our human logic, and we get ourselves in pits and valleys because of this. God asks us to trust Him when our vision is cloudy!

> *Trust in the LORD with all your heart, and do not lean on your own understanding. In all your ways acknowledge him, and he will make straight your paths.*
> —Prov. 3:5–6 ESV

He can see ahead to the thorny situations we could avoid. He wants to guide us away from trusting in the wrong spirits and to have us lean only on the Holy Spirit, who teaches truth!

> *Your word is a lamp to my feet and a light to my path. . . . The sum of your word is truth, and every one of your righteous rules endures forever.*
> —Ps. 119:105, 160 ESV

Can you trust God now for those things that you still don't understand?

Day Sixty-Three

*I am a little pencil in the hand of a writing God who is
sending a love letter to the world.*

—Mother Teresa

*Your very lives are a letter that anyone can read by just looking at you. Christ
himself wrote it—not with ink, but with God's living Spirit; not chiseled into
stone, but carved into human lives—and we publish it.*

—2 Cor. 3:1–3 MSG

What kind of message am I writing? What is the letter I'm writing into the lives
of those around me?

Is it a biting letter of criticism, a "woe is me" complaint, or is it an encouraging
love letter, a motivational note, and a sympathetic sentiment?

As Mother Teresa so sweetly explains, each of us is penning some kind of message to others. It's good to know that we can change our message if we aren't happy with what has been written so far!

We can enlist God's help in improving our flow of words to better express how we feel about those around us. We can allow God to guide our hand as we write our love letter to the world.

> *You will be a crown of splendor in the LORD's hand, a royal diadem in the hand of your God.*
>
> —Isa. 62:3 NIV

God is so patient and always ready to help us improve our writing skills. If what we've written so far needs a bit of tweaking, ask God to guide our minds and empower our hands to get the best message out to others!

> *It is the most amazing feeling to know how deeply You know me, inside and out; the realization of it is so great that I cannot comprehend it.*
>
> —Ps. 139:6 VOICE

What kind of letter have you been writing to those in your world?

Day Sixty-Four

The gem cannot be polished without friction, nor man perfected without trials.
—Seneca

Dear brothers and sisters, when troubles of any kind come your way,
consider it an opportunity for great joy.
—James 1:2

I don't have to tell you that life has its trials! They aren't very joyful in the moment! They can be as small as difficulties with your child, a rough patch with your spouse, or aches and pains that interrupt your day. They can be larger challenges as with money or health or a natural disaster that strikes!

I want to reassure you that although trials are difficult, they are common to us all and a necessary part of our growth. What is important is what happens in us when trials happen to us!

If we can make the wiser choice to draw near to God during these times and lean on His strength, His wisdom, and His leading, then the trial becomes an important phase of our growth!

> *For you know that when your faith is tested, your endurance has a chance to grow. So let it grow, for when your endurance is fully developed, you will be perfect and complete, needing nothing.*
>
> —James 1:3–4

We all understand how a small child will endure many bumps along their way to learn how to stand and walk. They fall off their bikes many times before they ride like the wind. Many mistakes and choices precede their path to wisdom.

We are like that as adults too. We have to go through the hard times to become aware and thankful for the good times.

The difficulties that come with learning to make better choices help us figure out that God is the one we can trust to provide the true strength and power to live a better life. We begin to trust in God's wisdom that will lead us to peace and joy.

> *You will keep in perfect peace all who trust in you, all whose thoughts are fixed on you!*
>
> —Isa. 26:3

When difficulties come, as they will come, can you trust what God is doing when you don't understand what is happening?

Day Sixty-Five

*The right word may be effective, but no word was ever as
effective as a rightly timed pause.*
—Mark Twain

*Understand this, my dear brothers and sisters: You must all be quick to listen,
slow to speak, and slow to get angry.*
—James 1:19

Listening is one of those skills that must be honed through lots of practice. I don't think most of us are adept at really listening. I know this is a problem for me. I mean really listening—giving pause to truly hear another's heart before I try to interject myself into the conversation!

If one gives answer before he hears, it is his folly and shame.
—Prov. 18:13 RSV

Often, we misunderstand someone's intentions; we make assumptions; we get upset and highly indignant too quickly all because we aren't really listening. The most wonderful gift we can give someone is the gift of being heard.

Most arguments, even while texting, happen because we hear with our bias; we read into their written words; we insert our inflections, or we misunderstand their intentions.

It always comes back to us! Will we really listen? Will we really hear? Will we truly "hear" their hearts in conversation? God's Word has much to advise us on the subject:

> *Fools have no interest in understanding; they only want to air their own opinions.*
>
> —Prov. 18:2

> *Even a fool who keeps silent is considered wise; when he closes his lips, he is deemed intelligent.*
>
> —Prov. 17:28 RSV

> *Watch your tongue and keep your mouth shut, and you will stay out of trouble.*
>
> —Prov. 21:23

> *The wise at heart will gladly obey direction, but one who fills the air with meaningless talk will fall into ruin.*
>
> —Prov. 10:8 VOICE

Can you place a greater emphasis on loving others by truly listening?

Day Sixty-Six

Courage is resistance to fear, mastery of fear, not absence of fear.
—Mark Twain

Even when I walk through the darkest valley, I will not be afraid, for you are close beside me. Your rod and your staff protect and comfort me.
—Ps. 23:4

Let's admit it! There are many things to be afraid of! And then for some of us, our imaginations can cause us to tremble over even more things that might happen to us or our loved ones. Whether you're a child lying in a dark room trying to sleep or a full-grown adult trying to get through the night, fear can be crippling!

Don't be afraid, for I am with you. Don't be discouraged, for I am your God. I will strengthen you and help you. I will hold you up with my victorious right hand.

—Isa. 41:10

If we could only equip our little ones with the confidence of God's Word when they are small. If we helped them recite scripture to guard and guide them when the fear of what's under the bed or in the corner grips their little minds, then just maybe, by adulthood, we'd all be ready to face the harder fears we encounter with faith!

I am holding you by your right hand—I, the Lord your God—and I say to you, Don't be afraid; I am here to help you.

—Isa. 41:13 TLB

We often arrive at adulthood trying to control our fears all by ourselves. Could this be why we fail to allow the Master to master our fears for us?

Let him have all your worries and cares, for he is always thinking about you and watching everything that concerns you.

—1 Pet. 5:7 TLB

Can you rest your head on your pillow with confidence and peace, trusting that God has you cradled in His care?

Day Sixty-Seven

I am an old man and have known a great many troubles,
but most of them never happened.
—Mark Twain

Therefore I tell you, do not be anxious about your life.
—Matt. 6:25 RSV

And which of you by being anxious can add a single hour to his span of life?
—Luke 12:25 ESV

Do you ever have a difficult time praying? Have you found prayer hardest during times of anxiety and fear? This is when we need prayer the most, and God wants us to grasp the reality that prayer and anxiety are diametrically opposed to each other.

While our thoughts are conjuring the "impossible, uncontrollable, helpless nature of the insecure aloneness of our situation," how can we at the same time talk to God and lean on His power and His provision?

The mind that is able to turn to prayer is a mind that has decided that no matter what, "God is there for me!" He is in control! He can bring light and a solution to my problem or my concern for someone that I love!

I trust His goodness, and I will patiently wait for Him to help me. In the meantime, I will search His Word, hold on to His character, remember His faithfulness in the past, and keep my mind in a thankful mode for what is still good in my life!

> *Gratitude—it helps you to see what is there—not what isn't!*
> —Annette Bridges

Let's see what is really there! God is there, God is able! God is bigger than any anxious thought we can imagine!

> *Let the peace that Christ gives control your thinking. It is for peace that you were chosen to be together in one body. And always be thankful.*
> —Col. 3:15 ERV

Can you ask God to give you the power to push away from anxiety and toward prayer?

Day Sixty-Eight

The success of love is in the loving—it is not in the result of loving.
—Mother Teresa

My children, our love should not be only words and talk. No, our love must be real. We must show our love by the things we do.
—1 John 3:18 ERV

When your efforts don't easily bring success, do you ever feel discouraged and want to give up on caring or including someone?

They may be hurting or have a loss; that may explain why they do not respond to you as you would like! To you, it seems easy to see what they need. When you try to help, they don't respond in appreciation as you'd expect.

I want to encourage you to keep on trying! Keep on loving for the sake of love! It's easy to justify pulling away because we aren't receiving the response that we think is fair. But may I call us to a higher purpose to love them as they need to be loved, not as they fail to understand love? We can ask God to give us the strength to keep on in our efforts.

Always be humble and gentle. Be patient and accept each other with love.
—Eph. 4:2 ERV

Often, the one who pushes us away is the one who is crying for love the most! Often, the hardest to love are the ones who need us to be the first one to patiently love them enough to break through their tough skin! Keep on loving! Who knows but that we could make an enemy a friend by our love!

"You have heard that it was said, 'Love your neighbor and hate your enemy.' But I tell you, love your enemies. Pray for those who treat you badly. If you do this, you will be children who are truly like your Father in heaven."
—Matt. 5:43–45 ERV

The Father has loved us so much! This shows how much he loved us: We are called children of God. And we really are his children.
—1 John 3:1 ERV

Who can you share love with today in response to Christ's great love for you?

Day Sixty-Nine

*The best and most beautiful things in this world cannot be
seen or even heard, but must be felt with the heart.*
—Helen Keller

Guard your heart with all vigilance, for from it are the sources of life.
—Prov. 4:23 NET

All Helen Keller's experiences of life were through her sense of touch. She did not allow loss of sight and hearing to prevent her from being shaped into a very beautiful, grateful, resourceful Christian role model for us of how to embrace a difficult life with joy!

Can you imagine being a small child, trying to learn and experience life without the ability to see and hear? How would we learn to talk or experience any other

person or understand why we are here on this earth or what beauty is or who loves you without these very important senses?

And yet Helen did! She has taught us that with perseverance in the worst of circumstances, the prison she was in could be broken through! She took what was left and made a beautiful life!

We too can focus on what we do have, not what we lack or what we've lost! We too, with the benefit of all our senses, can find the beauty of God's world like Helen did through touch! We too can bring it all into our hearts. We can feel deeply and appreciate all God has given us!

> *For where your treasure is, there your heart will be also.*
> —Matt. 6:21 NET

> *Your success and happiness lies [sic] within you. Resolve to keep happy, and your joy and you shall form an invisible force against difficulties.*
> —Helen Keller

> *Be delighted with the Lord. Then he will give you all your heart's desires.*
> —Ps. 37:4 TLB

How can you delight more in the senses God has given you?

Day Seventy

To the mind that is still, the whole universe surrenders.

Lao Tzu

Be still, and know that I am God!

—Ps. 46:10

Is it really possible to stop and be still? From the moment we awaken, we women are thinking, moving, planning, grooming, creating, exercising, cooking, cleaning, loving, teaching, working, making decisions. . . . In the midst of all that, is it really possible to stop and be still before God?

The LORD of Heaven's Armies is here among us.

—Ps. 46:11

If we really believe that our God is mighty, strong, sufficient, and powerful, we will stop and be still and wait for Him!

We don't really want to go into the fray alone without Him with us, do we? Whether we see our day as a battle or not, it is! Good and evil war for our hearts. Wisdom and foolishness vie for our time. Pains and pleasures may distract us from our higher purpose if we don't keep our greatest ally near to our hearts.

This morning: Be still! Just for a bit, stop and talk to your mighty Savior! Rest in His presence rather than rushing into the fray!

> *This is what the Sovereign LORD, the Holy One of Israel, says: "Only in returning to me and resting in me will you be saved. In quietness and confidence is your strength."*
>
> —Isa. 30:15

> *But the people who know their God shall be strong and do great things.*
>
> —Dan. 11:32 TLB

Can you stop, "be still," and listen to the Lord?

Day Seventy-One

One sees qualities at a distance and defects at close range.
—Victor Hugo

Hatred stirs up strife, but love covers and overwhelms all transgressions
[forgiving and overlooking another's faults].
—Prov. 10:12 AMP

Isn't it easy to find faults in others? They seem so glaring and often effectively cover over and hide virtues and abilities. We find it hard to understand, hard to look beyond to possible reasons why someone has certain failings!

It can even be our own sin that we see reflected in others' lives, which we so dislike. But we are far kinder when we see the same faults in ourselves.

I think if we can try to understand the difficulties from a person's past, such as who raised them, their disappointments, or the kind of life they suffered, maybe we can find it in our heart to love them. We might even be able to dig deeper into the well of our patience and cover them with God's grace, overlooking their flaws. Love does that so well!

After all, we were full of sin and failings when Jesus died in our place! Can't we die a little to ourselves instead of giving up on people because of their faults? Remember that we are one of those people too!

> *Above all, have fervent and unfailing love for one another, because love covers a multitude of sins [it overlooks unkindness and unselfishly seeks the best for others].*
>
> —1 Pet. 4:8 AMP

> *A person's wisdom yields patience; it is to one's glory to overlook an offense.*
> —Prov. 19:11 NIV

How can you overlook faults and notice the good qualities in others today instead?

Day Seventy-Two

Prayer should be the key of the day and the lock of the night.
—George Herbert

In the beginning the Word already existed.
The Word was with God, and the Word was God.
He existed in the beginning with God.
God created everything through him,
and nothing was created except through him.
The Word gave life to everything that was created,
and his life brought light to everyone.
The light shines in the darkness,
and the darkness can never extinguish it.

—John 1:1–5

Is there a lot going on in your world this day? I woke to the weight of many loved ones' needs, some weighty decisions that need to be made, and an unknown future for a friend due to illness. All this could weigh me down. But I've gotten in the wonderful pattern of making my very first action, after rising and getting my coffee, to be sitting with Jesus.

He is the Creator, He is here, He can be my boon companion as I begin this day. I share with Him all my deep concerns and give them over to Him. He carries the heavy weight of them for me so I can go on with my day!

I know I can trust His plan for each loved person I bring to Him! Jesus cares. After all, He died for each of them to live eternally with Him. That's why I know it's all going to be okay.

Jesus can be there with you too this day. Whatever is weighing you down, it doesn't have to sideline you! Jesus's presence can make all the difference for you too! Let Him sit in on whatever is happening, wherever you find yourself this day, and whoever is most in need!

> *We can come to God with no doubts. This means that when we ask God for things (and those things agree with what God wants for us), God cares about what we say. He listens to us every time we ask him. So we know that he gives us whatever we ask from him.*
> —1 John 5:14–15 ERV

What is weighing on your heart right now that you can bring to Jesus?

Day Seventy-Three

The single hand that wipes your tears during your failures is better than the countless hands that come together to clap you on your success.

—Nishan Panwar

You keep track of all my sorrows. You have collected all my tears in your bottle. You have recorded each one in your book.

—Ps. 56:8

It is so wonderful to be in the comforting arms of God during tough times—to know each tear is counted and cared about.

Maybe it's the times of waiting that have us searching out our Father's presence to help us cope when the waiting can seem so long. Or sometimes, it's the sting of hurt that has us running to our Savior's lap.

It often is our deep concern for our loved ones or friends whose plight we are laboring over that has us seeking God for answers and mercy!

Then very interestingly, that same comfort that we feel from our God inspires us to share, to pass on, to emulate His love, as we reach outward into the lives around us!

> *All praise to the God and Father of our Master, Jesus the Messiah! Father of all mercy! God of all healing counsel! He comes alongside us when we go through hard times, and before you know it, he brings us alongside someone else who is going through hard times so that we can be there for that person just as God was there for us.*
>
> —2 Cor. 1:3–5 MSG

> *May your loyal love console me, as you promised your servant. May I experience your compassion, so I might live!*
>
> —Ps. 119:76–77 NET

> *He heals the brokenhearted, and bandages their wounds.*
>
> —Ps. 147:3 NET

> *So speak encouraging words to one another. Build up hope so you'll all be together in this, no one left out, no one left behind. I know you're already doing this; just keep on doing it.*
>
> —1 Thess. 5:11 MSG

How can you take the love of God that you have experienced and pass that on to another today?

Day Seventy-Four

Hope is like the sun, which, as we journey toward it,
casts the shadow of our burden behind us.

—Samuel Smiles

Be happy because of the hope you have. Be patient when you have troubles.
Pray all the time.

—Rom. 12:12 ERV

Hope is both a choice and a confidence that we walk around displaying. Hope puts on a smile no matter what may be just under the surface of our day. Hope chooses to be thankful, grateful that even though one thing may be wrong at the moment, we have so much to look forward to—things that may occur today or tomorrow or next week or next year . . . !

Hope gets us outside of ourselves, so that we don't waste our precious moments complaining. Instead, we can be used to lift the moods of others who are struggling to find hope for themselves.

We can remind ourselves, and others, that God is here, God is good, and God has promises they can rely on. We can show them in His Word those wonderful hopeful verses that can keep sustaining them until Hope returns to their hearts again!

> *Everything that was written in the past was written to teach us. Those things were written so that we could have hope. That hope comes from the patience and encouragement that the Scriptures give us.*
>
> —Rom. 15:4 ERV

> *"I say this because I know the plans that I have for you." This message is from the* Lord. *"I have good plans for you. I don't plan to hurt you. I plan to give you hope and a good future."*
>
> —Jer. 29:11 ERV

As we pass by the mirror of our hearts, may we wear that inner smile of confident hope in expectation of God's many promises!

> *May the God of hope fill you with all joy and peace in believing, so that by the power of the Holy Spirit you may abound in hope.*
>
> —Rom. 15:13 RSV

How can you be more hopeful in your outlook today?

Day Seventy-Five

Adversity is the diamond dust heaven polishes its jewels with.
—Robert Leighton

Comfort and prosperity have never enriched the world as much as adversity has.
—Billy Graham

My brothers and sisters, you will have many kinds of trouble.
But this gives you a reason to be very happy. You know that when your faith is
tested, you learn to be patient in suffering. If you let that patience work in you,
the end result will be good. You will be mature and complete.
You will be all that God wants you to be.
—James 1:2–4 ERV

There is a reason for our struggles! There are unknown purposes for the troubles we encounter in life! They will always be for our polishing. They may well be to affect others in ways that words alone can't move!

Can we praise God and be thankful in times of adversity as much as in times when things are going smoothly? That's the real crux of the matter! Can we see God's loving hand through all the days, regardless of their content?

Are we letting God polish us to a glimmering shine? Are we hopeful no matter what? Today, let's take the path that leads to trust and hope!

> *But then I think about this, and I have hope: We are still alive because the Lord's faithful love never ends. Every morning he shows it in new ways! You are so very true and loyal! I say to myself, "The Lord is my God, and I trust him."*
>
> —Lam. 3:21–24 ERV

> *You keep him in perfect peace whose mind is stayed on you, because he trusts in you. Trust in the Lord forever, for the Lord God is an everlasting rock.*
>
> —Isa. 26:3–4 ESV

What adversity has taught you to hope more in God's strength for your struggles?

Day Seventy-Six

It's not what you look at that matters, it's what you see.
—Henry David Thoreau

It bears all things, believes all things, hopes all things, endures all things.
Love never ends.
—1 Cor. 13:7–8 NET

I've learned some valuable lessons when it comes to dealing with very difficult people. Sometimes, the problem involved someone on the world's stage or even someone close to me whom I was struggling with.

I may not agree in the way they handle things. It may be the way they think, or often, it's how they may treat others. It could just be the fact that when I want to help, they push away; this might cause a rift between us.

Amazingly, if I begin to pray for them and fervently ask God for good things for them, and if I dwell on all the things I like about them and allow that to be my focus instead of dwelling on the issue, my heart will feel better toward them.

They haven't changed at all—I have changed! My eyesight has been altered! In prayer, God can effect a change in my vision and in my heart's condition when it comes to seeing other people!

> *And he told them a parable, to the effect that they ought always to pray and not lose heart.*
>
> —Luke 18:1 RSV

> *Above all keep your love for one another fervent, because love covers a multitude of sins.*
>
> —1 Pet. 4:8 NET

Is there anyone in your life toward whom you should seek a heart change by beginning to pray for them?

Day Seventy-Seven

The happiness of your life depends upon the quality of your thoughts;
therefore, guard accordingly.

—Marcus Aurelius

You keep him in perfect peace whose mind is stayed on you,
because he trusts in you.

—Isa. 26:3 ESV

Choices, choices, choices! We have so many choices of what to consume each day. Food for the mind, I mean! Do I eat dessert all the time? Is my mind's diet all snacks—salty, spicy things—that can make me sick?

Do I fill my mind with silliness or, worse, horror and violence rather than beauty and meaning and value? What do I put into my mind? What goes in will come out in many, many ways!

Our dreams, our language, our behavior, our attitudes, and our conversations can be deeply shaped by what we consume. Are my fears heightened and my worries magnified by what I see and watch and read?

Just as the body is either helped or hurt by what we eat, so our minds can be distorted out of shape, or they can be made more like Christ's mind by our eating habits! Today, may I choose to examine how I feed my mind! My peace and joy and, yes, even my temporary happiness can be affected by it!

> *Whoever gives thought to the word will discover good, and blessed is he who trusts in the LORD.*
>
> —Prov. 16:20 ESV

What changes do you need to make to have a better diet for your mind today?

Day Seventy-Eight

A friend's eye is a good mirror.
—Celtic Proverb

The godly give good advice to their friends; the wicked lead them astray.
—Prov. 12:26

It is a good measure of our friendships if we can even pick one or two friends that we could ask this difficult, exposing question: "What do you see in me that needs to change so that I can be better?"

The heartfelt counsel of a friend is as sweet as perfume and incense.
—Prov. 27:9

Many will say they are loyal friends, but who can find one who is truly reliable?
—Prov. 20:6

The friend to whom I could ask that question would have to be a really close friend. That person would have been tested and tried so that I would trust that their response wouldn't be self-serving. They would have walked the road with me long enough to know what was needed to help me be a better person.

I can think of only a few trusted people with whom I might risk that question. But I might still be a bit afraid to hear what they think or say about my failings.

I do know of one friend to whom I can ask that question and not be afraid because I know the gentleness with which He would answer—the patient touch of His words that brings me life. He knows exactly how to tell me. He says it in a way that I will be able to handle! That friend is Jesus!

Jesus knocks at the door of our hearts. He patiently waits for the invitation to come and have those heartfelt conversations with us—the ones in which we ask him honestly to help us with our lives, our growth, and our future!

> *"Look! I stand at the door and knock. If you hear my voice and open the door,*
> *I will come in, and we will share a meal together as friends."*
>
> —Rev. 3:20

> *And this same God who takes care of me will supply all your needs from his*
> *glorious riches, which have been given to us in Christ Jesus.*
>
> —Phil. 4:19

Will you ask such a good friend as Jesus to help you make needed changes today?

Day Seventy-Nine

*Faith is the art of holding on to things your reason has once accepted,
in spite of your changing moods.*

—C. S. Lewis

*Dear brothers and sisters, when troubles of any kind come your way, consider it
an opportunity for great joy. For you know that when your faith is tested, your
endurance has a chance to grow. So let it grow, for when your endurance is
fully developed, you will be perfect and complete, needing nothing.*

—James 1:2–4

What do I have faith in? Who do I rely on? What do I trust in when times get challenging?

Life takes us through many ups and downs to test our answers to these questions. Then, we find out whom or what we rely on!

If we sat huddled in fear every time the darkness of night came, not believing we have illumination at our fingertips, we'd say that we had no faith in electricity! When trouble comes and we quake and fear as though we are all alone, then we have to question our faith in God's care.

But if trouble comes our way and we turn to our God and cry to Him for help, then we are more assured of our faith in Him. If His Word is tucked deep in our hearts and we know where to get sustaining scripture in a trial and find solace in His arms during troubled times, then the test of our faith proves genuine. If we know we can climb into His lap and rest rather than quake and tremble as though alone, then we can celebrate our trust in His goodness and protection.

Life's cement mixer will reveal whether our faith in God is real. Faith has to be tested so we'll know whether it needs some work! Is our faith just lip service, or is our faith in God something we can draw life and hope and strength from in times of trouble? Are we aware that God is there—the Light—at our fingertips? He is real and really available and strong enough and able to help us!

> *Fire tests the purity of silver and gold, but the LORD tests the heart.*
> —Prov. 17:3

Have you been tested lately? How have you done trusting God through it all?

Day Eighty

The only journey is the journey within.
—Rainer Maria Rilke

For the LORD your God has blessed you in everything you have done. He has watched your every step through this great wilderness. During these forty years, the LORD your God has been with you, and you have lacked nothing.
—Deut. 2:7

Have you ever felt that in this life, the journey has led us through many ups and downs and wanderings? We've fallen in pits, we've stepped on mountaintops, we've felt the highs and lows of life, and we've survived some close calls—perhaps even scrapes with death.

Is there the awareness and overwhelming joy in knowing, as I am aware, that the Lord has been with us all this time? He's rescued us from ourselves and from trouble. He's held us up in the frightening times. He's pulled us out of many pits of our own mistakes.

He's held our hand on the mountain vistas and celebrated the beauty of His creation in those high holy moments we experience when we are most aware of His presence. He reassures us in the trembling insecurities of our humanity, and He promises us that this journey will end in a very magnificent place that we can't even describe or imagine!

The journey within—wherever we go and whatever occurs—is the most important journey we will take! It's the journey with the Lord!

> *The LORD your God, who goes before you looking for the best places to camp, guiding you with a pillar of fire by night and a pillar of cloud by day.*
> —Deut. 1:32–33

Can you recall and thank God for how He has sustained you through your life's journey?

Day Eighty-One

Not the fastest horse can catch a word spoken in anger.
—Chinese Proverb

"I tell you that on the day of judgment, people will give an account for every worthless word they speak. For by your words you will be justified, and by your words you will be condemned."
—Matt. 12:36–37 NET

Tow often I have spoken out of turn. How often I've wasted words arguing over impossible subjects that have no end or solution and can lead to anger.

Death and life are in the power of the tongue, and those who love its use will eat its fruit.
—Prov. 18:21 NET

How often I've lost perspective and spoken carelessly or only about myself instead of taking the opportunity to learn more from a friend. Have you ever left a room or a conversation wondering if you said the wrong things? I have!

When I write each morning, God has the chance to get hold of my words and hone them to make His point. I can edit my words. I can remove and add in those inflections that communicate exactly what I mean.

But, in the moment, if I'm quick to speak and slow to listen, well then, it can all go wrong. I can hurt, I can bore, I can waste, I can gossip, or I can misunderstand. I don't want to do that!

I understand a bit better that each time I'm with a friend or a dear one, its precious time! It's a time to be meaningful, to explore, to find out more about them, to listen, and to care!

> *Understand this, my dear brothers and sisters! Let every person be quick to listen, slow to speak, slow to anger.*
>
> —James 1:19 NET

> *May my words and my thoughts be acceptable in your sight, O Lord, my sheltering rock and my redeemer.*
>
> —Ps. 19:14 NET

How are your listening skills?

Day Eighty-Two

Fear defeats more people than any other one thing in the world.
—Ralph Waldo Emerson

Don't be afraid, for I am with you. Don't be discouraged,
for I am your God. I will strengthen you and help you.
I will hold you up with my victorious right hand.

—Isa. 41:10

Fear can come without permission! Fear can dwell with us because we are busy dwelling on all our fears.

There are a lot of really awful things that could occur. If you are anything like I have been, then you've imagined every dire situation that could happen. I thought that thinking this way would prepare me for the worst. But this kind of thinking can drive you crazy!

Fretting, fearing—it's all because my thoughts are on me! It's implying that I am alone. I'm saying to myself, "I'm on my own!"

> *But when I am afraid, I will put my trust in you. I praise God for what he has promised. I trust in God, so why should I be afraid? What can mere mortals do to me?*
>
> —Ps. 56:3–4

God wants us to trust Him, to let His Word guard our thoughts, and to turn away from any tendency to think we are alone! He wants to remind us that He is with us! He is able!

He is willing and capable of carrying the weight of all our concerns! He wants us to be fully equipped to face our battles. He wants to quell our anxiety. He wants peace for us!

> *Don't worry about anything; instead, pray about everything; tell God your needs, and don't forget to thank him for his answers. If you do this, you will experience God's peace, which is far more wonderful than the human mind can understand. His peace will keep your thoughts and your hearts quiet and at rest as you trust in Christ Jesus.*
>
> —Phil. 4:6–7 TLB

Is there a worry you need to bring to God and leave in His capable hands?

Day Eighty-Three

I don't worry about being in a hurry anymore,
because my faith in God will always deliver me on time.
—Martha Reeves

Come to me, all you who are weary and burdened, and I will give you rest.
Take my yoke on you and learn from me, because I am gentle and humble in
heart, and you will find rest for your souls.
—Matt. 11:28–29 NET

I believe that being in such a hurry is a modern-day problem. Maybe the possibility that we can accomplish so much in a day in our fast-paced world increases our expectations for what we can accomplish.

Without leaving my home, I can get anything delivered as soon as tomorrow from Amazon! I can travel on wonderful connecting roads in fast machines that get me anywhere in record time these days!

Whatever my mind questions, "Hey Google" or "Siri" can find out for me. I don't even need a cookbook; even standing in the grocery store, I can search and find any recipe and be on my way. I can have food delivered to my door, "lickety-split"!

When I think back to the slower pace before the industrial revolution, news took many days or weeks to travel; buying provisions was an entire day's ride. Travel was a whole different experience long ago!

Getting information or even finding a bound book was so different then compared to the convenience of apps on our phones that can deliver any novel, any wisdom—almost anything we desire!

How, Lord, can we have time for you with all this distraction? How, Lord, can we put aside our expectations for a day so that we can just stop and rest? How, Lord, can we need you when every need seems to be met already in other ways!

Oh, Lord, can we slow our pace? Help us, Lord, to put down our devices, shut off the noise, take a walk and think, go out and play, go inward and pray, and trust You more!

He says, "Stop your striving and recognize that I am God! I will be exalted over the nations! I will be exalted over the earth!"

—Ps. 46:10 NET

How can you slow down and take some time away to connect with God?

Day Eighty-Four

First mend yourself, then mend others.
—Jewish Proverb

Now your attitudes and thoughts must all be constantly changing for the better.
—Eph. 4:23 TLB

It is so much easier to see the faults and failings in others than in ourselves, don't you think? I'm sure you could tell me quickly some great ideas on what could help your spouse, a friend, or your boss be a better person!

It's built into us naturally to be kinder to ourselves and more critical of others. We more easily notice failings and faults in others, and just as easily forgive or are blind to our own. It takes a supernatural desire to refocus our minds on self-improvement and have the heart to extend charity toward others.

Self-improvement is not selfishness. Seeking to glorify God by cleaning out the detritus of hidden faults and not-so-hidden failings is a good kind of self-focus! It also solves the problem of being critical toward others.

If I am humble in my attitude about myself, then I will have a more realistic and kinder view of others too! If my attention is on improving my own house, then I will not be noticing and critical of another's abode.

> *Don't copy the behavior and customs of this world, but let God transform you into a new person by changing the way you think. Then you will learn to know God's will for you, which is good and pleasing and perfect.*
> —Rom.12:2

Will you ask God to reveal any changes needed so that you can have a clearer view of yourself and a kinder assessment of others?

Day Eighty-Five

We have to start teaching ourselves not to be afraid.
—William Faulkner

When anxiety overtakes me and worries are many,
your comfort lightens my soul.
—Ps. 94:19 VOICE

What I remember about William Faulkner isn't much more than some memorized facts about a Nobel Prize winner for literature. When I studied his life, I understood better why he wrote this quote.

His life was full of losses, fits and starts, the "almost," and not any real sense of success until later in his life. He was like most of us, venturing forward with dreams, talents, and no idea of whether he could fulfill them in this big world.

The real truth of the matter is that we are not alone! We don't have to fight the tendency to fear; the overpowering feelings of worry and anxiety need not put us in isolation and doubt. God is here for us at every moment of our life, every instance of our need.

Just as our breathing shallows and we gasp in times of anxiety, so too we seem to seize up and forget what we know: God is for us, God is with us, God is in us, ALWAYS!

Take a deep breath, remember your Word, let it all sink down deep into your heart—that God is real, God is able, God is willing to walk us through and equip us completely for every moment of our day and our life!

> *Don't be afraid, for I am with you! Don't be frightened, for I am your God! I strengthen you—yes, I help you—yes, I uphold you with my saving right hand!*
> —Isa. 41:10 NET

> *Do not be anxious about anything. Instead, in every situation, through prayer and petition with thanksgiving, tell your requests to God. And the peace of God that surpasses all understanding will guard your hearts and minds in Christ Jesus.*
> —Phil. 4:6–7 NET

What has you in a grip of fear today?
Will you allow God to give you the peace He offers?

Day Eighty-Six

We are twice armed if we fight with faith.

—Plato

So be strong and courageous! Do not be afraid and do not panic before them.
For the LORD your God will personally go ahead of you.
He will neither fail you nor abandon you.

—Deut. 31:6

Are you in a battle today? I believe in some way, for someone, we are. We may be seeking help with illness, asking for healing for a loved one, needing a change in health, feeling concern for a child at school, seeking a better job, wanting freedom from bad habits, or fervently wishing for better friendships. Faith is needed to see that we are not alone!

We aren't praying into the air. We aren't just hopefully wishing on a star. No, we have the powerful God of the universe in our corner!

Our prayers are heard by God in heaven. Our words are often the battle cry for angelic intervention in the fight for good to triumph over evil, for healing, for love, or for comfort in loss. Believe!

> *This is the confidence we have in approaching God: that if we ask anything according to his will, he hears us. And if we know that he hears us—whatever we ask—we know that we have what we asked of him.*
>
> —1 John 5:14–15 NIV

Trusting God's goodness and loving concern for you is number one in this fight. Know that He is leading the charge for you—He's on your side!

We aren't alone as we process hard news, as we fear for another, as we face a dark day, or when we have great success on our happiest days! He's there for it all!

Let Him in. Let Him wait with you. Let Him carry you. Let Him intercede for you. Don't try to carry your burden alone! It's too heavy alone!

> *Keep on asking, and you will receive what you ask for. Keep on seeking, and you will find. Keep on knocking, and the door will be opened to you.*
>
> —Matt. 7:7

What can you turn over to God today and allow Him to fight for you?

Day Eighty-Seven

Let your hopes not your hurts shape your future.
—Robert H. Schuller

And let the peace that comes from Christ rule in your hearts. For as members of one body you are called to live in peace. And always be thankful.
—Col. 3:15

What do I dwell on? There is a big price for dwelling on the hurts done to me. Harboring hurt often doesn't affect the one who disappointed me or maligned me at all. They may never really know how I feel!

But, for me, it chips away at my peace. It saps my happiness in the moment and messes with my attitude. I can't think about thankfulness when I harbor hurt! It filters out the good words and replaces them with complaint and negativity.

In short, un-forgiveness ruins my future hopeful possibilities. Oh, I can fool myself into thinking that it doesn't matter a bit. But, deep down, holding on to hurts can sicken my soul.

> *If you forgive those who sin against you, your heavenly Father will forgive*
> *you. But if you refuse to forgive others, your Father will not forgive your sins.*
> —Matt. 6:14–15

In fact, if I don't let go of the hurt and clean out my heart, it hurts my friendship with God! I don't want that! After all, Jesus gave His very life's blood to forgive me all my failings and sin.

How can I not see that it is far better for me, far easier in the long run, to give my hurt up and let it go if my goal is to live a joyful and full life. May I not hold on to anything negative. I'm only hurting myself!

Often, it's our closest relationships where un-forgiveness dwells! The person who offended me may not even be around anymore, and we still hold things against them! Is there anything keeping God from forgiving our failings? Anyone we are refusing to forgive? Let's let it go for our own sakes!

Who have you withheld forgiveness from, and in so doing, robbed your own heart of peace?

Day Eighty-Eight

"Jeremiah, say to the people, 'This is what the LORD *says: "When people fall down, don't they get up again? When they discover they're on the wrong road, don't they turn back?"'*
—Jer. 8:4

Children provide a good illustration for determination. I can't imagine a toddler not moving from creeping, to crawling, to standing, and then to stepping and walking.

It's a long tough battle from our vantage point. For them, it's such an instinctive process. Children just wake up each day, ready to go, ready to strive for more progress, hungering for the next step toward freedom.

What happens to us? Are we more likely to sit and complain about all the reasons we can't do something? Will we lie in our beds fearing the next hurdle rather than popping up with determination for the day?

What do I need to do to become more motivated? Do I ask God for help? Do I feel alone in my struggles? Because that isn't the truth—and I know it, really!

Just like the little toddler has a parent or two who are encouraging them in their attempts, I have a Heavenly Father with His arms out wide saying, "Come on, you can do it!" "Come to Papa. That's right, sweetheart, pull yourself up. You can do it! Don't give up. Try it again!"

> *Trust the LORD completely, and don't depend on your own knowledge. With every step you take, think about what he wants, and he will help you go the right way.*
>
> —Prov. 3:5–6 ERV

> *He brought me up out of a horrible pit [of tumult and of destruction], out of the miry clay, and He set my feet upon a rock, steadying my footsteps and establishing my path. He put a new song in my mouth, a song of praise to our God; many will see and fear [with great reverence] and will trust confidently in the LORD.*
>
> —Ps. 40:2–3 AMP

What can you ask your "Papa" to give you the courage to attempt?

Day Eighty-Nine

However beautiful the strategy, you should occasionally look at the results.
—Winston Churchill

Let your eyes look directly forward, and your gaze be straight before you. Take heed to the path of your feet, then all your ways will be sure.
—Prov. 4:25–26 RSV

Every once in a while, maybe even every day, we can analyze the time and energy we put into each of our activities. We often find ourselves on a wheel spinning in circles, like a mouse does—very busy, very active, but accomplishing what?

We could ask ourselves several thought-provoking questions. Is what I am involved in the best choice of activity that will move me closer to God? Am I doing nice things, but have I lost the compelling reason I've been doing these nice things?

Am I involved in good works out of gentle coercion, or am I truly passionate and excited about each good work I do? Am I doing only what I want to do, or am I seeking what God has prepared for me?

This assessment may require some alone time and some prayer to get reenergized and be reminded of God's Word. It may take planning to let some things go so you can make room for healthier choices. Let God in to whisper to you what He wants you to make time for!

> *Trust in and rely confidently on the LORD with all your heart and do not rely on your own insight or understanding. In all your ways know and acknowledge and recognize Him, and He will make your paths straight and smooth [removing obstacles that block your way].*
> —Prov. 3:5–6 AMP

Is there something for which you've lost the joy, and that letting it go could make time for something better?

Day Ninety

Ever tried. Ever failed. No matter. Try again.
Fail again. Fail better.

—Samuel Beckett

But as for you, be strong and courageous,
for your work will be rewarded.

—2 Chron. 15:7

Do you get discouraged easily when your efforts don't bring success? How has your attitude affected your ability to keep on going? Have you been able to keep getting up and trying again? Have you given up on something or someone because of this?

I have been that person! In those moments of trying and failing, I have felt all alone. Now I know better that I am not alone. Now I realize that I didn't have all the tools I could have had at my disposal. I had not even made the attempt that might just have brought success.

I failed to ask God for His help! I know it may seem obvious to you, but in those discouraging moments of failing, it's so easy to forget that He is there for me, with me, and in me!

He is saying to me: "I will never fail you. I will never abandon you" (Heb. 13:5). So, rather than listening to my own discouraging voice, I turn to Him! My Papa, my Father, my Companion, my Counselor, my God! If I ask, He will even be there ahead of me.

> The LORD himself goes before you and will be with you; he will never leave
> you nor forsake you. Do not be afraid; do not be discouraged.
> —Deut. 31:8 NIV

So, trust God. Ask for His help and believe He is going ahead to prepare the way for eventual success!

Have you thought to ask God for His help in this situation?

Day Ninety-One

Love, like a river, will cut a new path whenever it meets an obstacle.
—Crystal Middlemas

Love never gives up, never loses faith, is always hopeful,
and endures through every circumstance.
—1 Cor. 13:7

Whether a hidden roof leak or flooding rain, water will always find its way. It will course and weave. It will go around and find its way through as though drawn by a magnet.

Can love be as determined as water to flow through every difficult path and just as determined to be poured forth? Difficult people, hateful attitudes, impatient drivers, small minds, stubborn hearts, or cranky children: these are some of the many obstacles we meet in our attempts to pour out love.

But we can be determined to be people who continue to find a path toward love, can't we? We can take those circuitous routes to paths of kindness, forgiveness, and patience that will find their openings to let love flow.

We can be the people who keep trying, who resist reacting to pride and boasting, deflect lies, turn from fear, and overlook discouraging remarks. These are like dams in our path to love!

We can do it. We can strive to keep love coursing its way through our day!

> *This is love: not that we loved God, but that he loved us and sent his Son as an atoning sacrifice for our sins. Dear friends, since God so loved us, we also ought to love one another.*
>
> —1 John 4:10–11 NIV

Is love flowing through you, or are there obstacles that need your attention?

Day Ninety-Two

It is not enough to take steps which may someday lead to a goal;
each step must be itself a goal and a step likewise.
—Johann Wolfgang von Goethe

Teach us how short our lives are so that we can become wise. . . . Fill us with
your love every morning. Let us be happy and enjoy our lives.
—Ps. 90:12, 14 ERV

I have wasted valuable, and what could have been the sweetest, moments because my vision was elsewhere. It was inward, pondering my fears, or it was off in the distance wishing for something beyond this moment. How sad it is not to see the preciousness of this day because of the wistfulness of *ennui*.

I was chatting with a friend who had actually died—until his wife revived his heart while waiting for the EMS to come. Now, after a long recovery, he says his perspective on life has been altered completely. He's thinking differently about every moment and every person in his life—even thinking about how he spends his time and what is more important than where his focus was before.

I want to live this way too, don't you? I want to make every moment sweet, hold tightly to those I love, and care more about many more people in my world. I want to think more deeply about what God wants me to be and do for Him. I want to take every step and mark that moment as everything for that moment.

I want to have my eyes really open and aware, being observant and caring for each person, each creature, and each beautiful view that God has given me to witness today—right now, in this moment.

Then if I can string all these moments together, that will be a precious life to live, won't it?

> *I say this because you know that we live in an important time. Yes, it is now time for you to wake up from your sleep. Our salvation is nearer now than when we first believed.*
>
> —Rom. 13:11 ERV

How have you been living each of your days?

Day Ninety-Three

Conversation is food for the soul.
—Mexican Proverb

Kind words are like a life-giving tree.
—Prov. 15:4 ERV

One of the wonderful traits most women share is that we love a good conversation. Sharing ourselves with close girlfriends or getting back in sync with our sisters is just a feast of words.

We can literally lose our voices and lose sleep in the hours and days of a visit! I imagine it is good for the body to connect heart to heart. After a good visit, we may come back worn out but not worn down. Just the opposite. We feel understood, connected, hopeful, and inspired!

Can our conversations with God be even better and deeper than those with other people? I believe they can be. We don't have to wait for only special times to visit with God. We don't have to wear out our voices.

We can connect heart to heart with our God at any moment of our day and night. Before we are fully awake, we can begin our morning chat and keep it going, sharing our mountains and valleys, our hopes and dreams, our fervent wishes and deepest concerns with our dear Father, our precious Savior, our comforting Holy Spirit companion. We can know that we are heard, understood, valued, and validated at every tick of the day's clock.

We can drive with Him, we can fly with Him, and we can wait for that news with Him. He promises to be with us when we cry and when we sing; he'll work right alongside us.

Our meals can be with Him, and we can even play with Him by our side! He can be our closest friend who understands without explaining, who cares the most, and who loves us regardless of our ups and downs of failure and success!

And sometimes, there just are no words, and yet He knows what our hearts are saying and can pray for us when words are just too much for us!

And the Father who knows all hearts knows, of course, what the Spirit is saying as he pleads for us in harmony with God's own will.
—Rom. 8:27 TLB

Have you found joy in sharing a heart-to-heart with your dear Lord?

Day Ninety-Four

*Astronomy compels the soul to look upwards and
leads us from this world to another.*

—Plato

*Sun and moon, praise him! Stars and lights in the sky, praise him! Praise him,
highest heaven! Waters above the sky, praise him!*

—Ps. 148:3–4 ERV

I remember stretching out under the stars as a child. We'd lie in the cool grass and gaze up at the dark sky filled to brimming with twinkling lights. We'd watch for shooting stars to make a wish on and marvel at the mystery and the awesomeness of it all. My thoughts would turn and look higher than my little world and family to wonder about the God who made all this and more!

If you've ever been up before dawn and watched those first hints of pink and gold piercing the dark sky and watched the colors changing to bring out the morning sunlight, you know that it is an amazing sight. So too are the sunset, the drama of a storm, the breathtaking quiet and blinding white vistas of the snowy mountains, the overwhelming sight of the Grand Canyon, or the red rocks of Sedona.

God certainly thought of us, His beloved creation, when He took so much time to create such beauty—for us! Thank you, Creator God, for the beauty and wonder of Your natural world. May our minds and hearts soar to think of You and thank You, praising You for such a gift!

> *I look at the heavens you made with your hands. I see the moon and the stars you created. And I wonder, "Why are people so important to you? Why do you even think about them? Why do you care so much about humans? Why do you even notice them?"*
>
> —Ps. 8:3–4 ERV

> *Praise him, young men and women, old people and children. Praise the LORD's name! Honor his name forever! His name is greater than any other. He is more glorious than heaven and earth.*
>
> —Ps. 148:12–13 ERV

Have you noticed the beautiful gift of nature lately?

Day Ninety-Five

Nobody has ever measured, not even the poets, how much the heart can hold.
—Zelda Fitzgerald

Only the Lord knows! He searches all hearts and examines deepest motives so he can give to each person his right reward, according to his deeds—how he has lived.
—Jer. 17:10 TLB

We'd like to think we understand our own heart. Our feelings, as capricious as they can be, wax and wane with the tides. We'd like to think we could even control our hearts and how they react to circumstances, to other people's whims, to unexpected hurts, or passionate responses.

God tells us that the heart can't really be understood at all—by anyone but Him! Haven't we tried before and learned that this is true? One thing He does tell us is that we can be sure that wherever our heart is, that will be where our energy, our focus, and even our worship will be!

> *For where your treasure is, there your heart will be also.*
> —Matt. 6:21 NIV

Because I know this now, I want to be careful with my time, my mind, my energy, my hopes, and my heart. I want to put my heart into what matters to God and let my heart be guided by God.

> *Trust in the LORD with all your heart and lean not on your own understanding.*
> —Prov. 3:5 NIV

God can protect me from being confused and misled by whims! I know that whatever is in my heart will eventually come from my lips and affect the choices I make!

> *Search me, O God, and know my heart; test me and know my anxious thoughts. Point out anything in me that offends you, and lead me along the path of everlasting life.*
> —Ps. 139:23–24

Have you too found this true about your heart—that it is beyond your understanding?

Day Ninety-Six

Love is a fruit in season at all times, and within reach of every hand.
—Mother Teresa

Dear friends, let us practice loving each other, for love comes from God and those who are loving and kind show that they are the children of God, and that they are getting to know him better.
—1 John 4:7 TLB

Driving through central Florida, you pass acres and acres of orange groves. The growers must wait in expectation each year to harvest their orange crops. It's the lifeblood of their business. The fragrant juice is extracted and sold to make a really wonderful nutritious drink most of us enjoy.

Can you imagine if their trees just kept producing all year, at all times? That is the way love is. We don't have to sit idle, in neutral, waiting for just the special times to express love to others. God asks us to pick the fruit of love and share it with everyone and anyone.

The fruit of love is low hanging, in reach, and abundant. We can give it away to the cranky driver, the difficult neighbor, the sweet older people in nursing homes, the child we encounter running through our yards, the teen with the tats, the tough boss, and the homeless on our city streets.

We can overflow with a bushel of love to our husbands and our children; we can put the fruit in laps of strangers we brush by during our days. The wonderful thing about love is we don't need to be sparing with it, thinking there won't be enough to go around. No, amazingly, the more fruit we pick and share, the more our tree will bear.

Love will be overflowing into our laps! God will bless us beyond measure!

Give to others, and you will receive. You will be given much. It will be poured into your hands—more than you can hold. You will be given so much that it will spill into your lap. The way you give to others is the way God will give to you.

—Luke 6:38 ERV

So, pick the fruit of love and spread it around generously!
Anyone you know today who needs a bushel of love?

Day Ninety-Seven

Don't make a mountain out of a molehill.
—English Proverb

Many hardships and perplexing circumstances confront the righteous,
*But the L*ORD *rescues him from them all.*
—Ps. 34:19 AMP

What if we changed our perspective about trouble? What if, instead of being surprised at little or bigger things that go wrong in a day, we are rather elated and grateful when our day runs smoothly?

If we were to prepare our hearts for each day by being on guard for whatever may come and putting in place encouraging, reminding words to help us adjust to any unpleasant surprises, then maybe we would sail through our days with more joy. We

can use words like these: "God, you give true peace to people who depend on you, to those who trust in you" (Isa. 26:3 ERV).

And this could guard our hearts and remind us of Jesus's promise: "I leave you peace. It is my own peace I give you. I give you peace in a different way than the world does. So don't be troubled. Don't be afraid" (John 14:27 ERV).

We might take a bit more time to plan our day, adding extra time for travel when the roads are full, slowing down a bit while shopping, and taking into account the longer checkout lines. If we could understand the tension of others who are less prepared and show kindness, then we'd have a profoundly altered shopping season, wouldn't we?

> *Let your reasonableness be known to everyone. The Lord is at hand; do not be anxious about anything, but in everything by prayer and supplication with thanksgiving let your requests be made known to God. And the peace of God, which surpasses all understanding, will guard your hearts and your minds in Christ Jesus.*
>
> —Phil. 4:5–7 ESV

Doesn't that just sound like a better way to start this day?

Day Ninety-Eight

The teacher has not taught until the student has learned.
—English Proverb

Such things were written in the Scriptures long ago to teach us.
And the Scriptures give us hope and encouragement as we wait patiently for
God's promises to be fulfilled.
—Rom. 15:4

My heart goes out to all the teachers I had when I was a child. Very few really were effective in passing on their learning to me. I was so shy and fearful as a small child. Moving and changing schools might have contributed to my difficulties.

I do remember bright moments in high school. I had a wonderful math teacher and loved this subject. I also recall how important and freeing it was to be taught

sewing and cooking skills in home economics class. I retained much of what those teachers tried to instill in me.

Most of us don't realize the great opportunity learning is at the time. Now I do hunger for knowledge. How about you? Have you continued to learn and grow?

One book above all others that is so valuable to learn from is the Bible. Its words are alive. Have you felt that mysterious pull as you have read the scriptures in these devotionals? If they have touched and stimulated your heart and resolve, then you understand how God's Word works in our lives.

I want you to take God words with you into your home and day. They are the flashlight to illuminate our path in the dark times that befall us—those times when fear, insecurity, sickness, maladies, strong emotions, and even the high points of our lives happen. Those are the times when we want to draw wisdom and strength from somewhere, from someone.

We find in these words and moments that God cares for us and that He longs to help us make sense out of this life.

> *God's word is alive and working. It is sharper than the sharpest sword and cuts all the way into us. It cuts deep to the place where the soul and the spirit are joined. God's word cuts to the center of our joints and our bones. It judges the thoughts and feelings in our hearts.*
>
> —Heb. 4:12 ERV

Has God's Word spoken to your heart?
What is its message for you to learn today?

Day Ninety-Nine

*My mother said, "Don't worry about what people think now. Think about
whether your children or grandchildren will think you've done well."*
—Lord Mountbatten

*Each generation will praise you and tell the next
generation about the great things you do.*
—Ps. 145:4 ERV

There is something about having children in our lives that reminds us and invites
us to take stock of who we have been, what we are about, what is important to
us, and where we are headed.

I believe that God builds this into the lives of families, that even if we've been
clueless early on, when children arrive, we begin to look at life through their eyes,

beyond ourselves, into their futures. It changes us. When those little eyes look up to us, think so highly of us, and seek to emulate our ways, it gives us pause to consider, "How am I acting?" "What is my witness to them?" "What do they see that is most important to me?"

Those we influence may come directly or indirectly into our lives. They come through bearing them, adopting them, through our children's friendships, through our sisters' and brothers' children. But they do come, and they do seek us out as role models.

What kind of legacy are we leaving for them? What kind of message are we relating about life, about God and faith, about work, and about love?

> *We will not hide these truths from our children; we will tell the next generation about the glorious deeds of the LORD, about his power and his mighty wonders.*
>
> —Ps. 78:4

> *But from everlasting to everlasting the LORD's love is with those who fear him, and his righteousness with their children's children.*
>
> —Ps. 103:17 NIV

Have you considered the legacy you are leaving for those who look up to you?

Day One Hundred

If there is to be any peace it comes through being, not having.
—Henry Miller

I listen carefully to what God the LORD is saying, for he speaks peace to his faithful people. But let them not return to their foolish ways.
—Ps. 85:8

When I was in college living in my hometown, Pensacola, the local radio station would have a treasure hunt each year. I was always so hopeful that I could ferret out the strange clues and find the cache of gold.

I recall how we'd drive all over trying to break the codes and be the ones to solve the puzzle given out each week. We'd end up out on the beach where the clues usually took us, and we would drive and hike all over the sand dunes (back when we were

allowed on the sand dunes). I never did find that treasure; although I spent a great deal of time trying to and dreaming about what kind of bounty it could be.

Life is so much like that treasure hunt. The search for things consumes us. The challenge and hunt for success, possessions, career opportunities, financial growth, popularity, notoriety, and social status can fill up our minds and our time. In the end, what have we got?

What we want in the end more than anything is freedom from all that striving. Can I get an Amen? Something much deeper draws our hearts. We seek meaning of it all and a deeper value and purpose for the rest of our lives.

> *Stop doing anything evil, and do good. Look for peace, and do all you can to help people live peacefully.*
>
> —Ps. 34:14 ERV

So, I want to take the same energy I put into seeking earthly treasure that, in the end, failed me and pour it all instead into the pursuit of treasure that will last!

> *God's kingdom is like a treasure hidden in a field. One day a man found the treasure. He hid it again and was so happy that he went and sold everything he owned and bought the field.*
>
> —Matt. 13:44 ERV

What kind of treasure have you been seeking?

For whatever things were written before were written for our learning,
that through perseverance and through encouragement of the
Scriptures we might have hope.

—Rom. 15:4 WEB

About the Author

Barbara Maxwell was born in Patuxent River, Maryland, but she spent most of her childhood in Pensacola, Florida. Graduating with a degree in marketing from the University of West Florida in 1973, Barbara served as senior class president and was elected to Who's Who Among Students.

Having grown up with six sisters and a brother, Barbara has a heart for the unique challenges that women face. She and her husband, Mike, have been married for 44 years, and she is the mother of two grown daughters and the proud grandmother of several grandchildren.

Her longing to encourage women led to her daily devotional ministry. Barbara's faith has been seasoned with years of study and a circuitous route through various Christian faith experiences.

Barbara loves reading, cooking, exploring creative arts, and spending time with her daughters, grandchildren, and friends. She also enjoys spending time in Bible study, writing devotionals, and singing with her guitar-playing husband. She and her husband live in one of the most beautiful places in Florida, Miromar Lakes.

Acknowledgments

Thank you, Judy Teeven, for your friendship. You have taught me to believe in myself and inspired me to reach higher.

Thank you to my husband, Mike, who has loved me, been my barista, and provided constant encouragement to me each morning as I write.

Amy and Laura, my sweet daughters—you have always been close to my heart. Because of you, I am inspired to keep writing.

Thank you to all my texting group of sisters, daughters, and friends, and even a few great guys too. You know who you are! I'm forever grateful to you for your loyalty and encouragement to me over the years.

Thank you to all my many godly teachers who have guided my study and helped me dig deeper and reach higher in my knowledge of God and His Word.

First and last, I thank my God for the deep mystery of You—the Father, Son, and Holy Spirit. I would have been lost without Your daily nourishment, inspiration, guidance, and ability to do in me what would have been impossible for me before— to write!

CPSIA information can be obtained
at www.ICGtesting.com
Printed in the USA
LVHW101158270820
664241LV00051B/477